The **BIG BOOK** of
Baseball
BRAINTEASERS

The BIG BOOK of Baseball BRAINTEASERS

DOM FORKER, WAYNE STEWART,
& ROBERT OBOJSKI

Main Street
A division of Sterling Publishing Co., Inc.
New York

Library of Congress Cataloging-in-Publication Data Available

2 4 6 8 10 9 7 5 3

Published by Sterling Publishing Co., Inc.
387 Park Avenue South, New York, NY 10016

This book is comprised of material from the following Sterling titles:
Big League Baseball Puzzlers © 1991 by Dom Forker
Baseball Bafflers © 1999 by Wayne Stewart
Baseball's Zaniest Moments © 1999 by Rob Obojski

© 2004 by Sterling Publishing Co., Inc.
Distributed in Canada by Sterling Publishing
c/o Canadian Manda Group, 165 Dufferin Street
Toronto, Ontario, Canada M6K 3H6
Distributed in Great Britain by Chrysalis Books Group PLC
The Chrysalis Building, Bramley Road, London W10 6SP, England
Distributed in Australia by Capricorn Link (Australia) Pty. Ltd.
P.O. Box 704, Windsor, NSW 2756, Australia

Sterling 1-4027-1337-1

Contents

With *The Big Book of Baseball Brainteasers*, your baseball knowledge will become hall-of-fame worthy. While some of the trivia in this book might throw even the biggest baseball fanatic a curve ball, undoubtedly, you will discover fun facts about the game, test your baseball smarts, and learn what some of the greatest players had to say about America's pastime.

Unlike other trivia books, *The Big Book of Baseball Brainteasers* does not just toss around stats. Rather, this book even takes a look at fun facts and memorable moments off the field from the dugout to the press box and on the road. For example, did you know the average life of a major league baseball is six pitches? And the thirty teams of Major League Baseball use 720,000 baseballs each season, all of which are made by hand? For more on the history of the baseball, flip to pages 30-31.

Besides considering memorable moments, *The Big Book of Baseball Brainteasers* is unique because it deconstructs plays—actual and hypothetical—examining the players, the legality, and the consequences of all types of plays from the batter's box to the outfield to the officials. For example, is it legal if a baseman asks a player to step off the base so that he can clean it, and then tags the runner out? (The answer is yes, if the baseman has the ball and the umpire knows he has the ball, see Hidden Ball, Part I page 122.)

In addition to exploring the personalities and sportsmanship of baseball, this book examines the rules and technicalities of the game. For instance, what is the height of the pitcher's mound, can it be altered? (It's ten inches for all teams; for the complete rule, see page 97.) Or is play during a fog out, bug out, or black out treated differently from a rain out? For all three situations, the answer for is no, if you cannot see the ball, then the game is suspended, pages 250-51.

So on your favorite team's off days and during the off season, brush up on your baseball lore, familiarize yourself with the intricacies of the rulebook, and the get to know the game's greatest legends!

CHAPTER 1

At Bat

Not Joe DiMaggio

Some people claim that umpires give certain players the benefit of the doubt: Joe DiMaggio and Ted Williams, for example, Wade Boggs and Tony Gwynn, too.

Skeeter Newsome, an infielder for the Philadelphia Athletics, was at the plate one day when umpire Bill McGowan called him out on a close pitch after a three-two count. Newsome's pride was injured. "You wouldn't have called (Joe) DiMaggio out on that pitch," he resentfully said.

"You're darn right I wouldn't," McGowan shot back. "He would have hit it off that 457-foot sign in left-center field."

Was It a Strike?

One night Richie Ashburn complained about a strike call to home-plate umpire Jocko Conlan.

"Okay," Jocko said, "I'll let you umpire and hit at the same time."

Ashburn initially was reluctant, but he finally agreed. "Okay," he said.

The next pitch was two inches inside. Ashburn hesitated in his call of the pitch, and then finally said, "Strike."

"Strike!" Conlan half yelled and questioned at the same time. Then he took off his cap and dusted the plate. Finally he said to Ashburn, "You had the first and only chance in history to hit and umpire at the same time, and you blew it. No more. I'm not going to let you give umpiring a bad name. From now on you're just a hitter."

Hit Your Cutoff Man

When Dave Winfield was with the San Diego Padres, he once went through a bad stretch of games in which he had difficulty hitting his cutoff man.

Shortly after a workout focusing on hitting cutoffs, Winfield had a chance to snap out of his defensive woes. On a hard-hit single to the outfield, Winfield quickly and smoothly came up with the ball in shallow center field.

Darrell Thomas lined himself up with Winfield to take the throw. But, since he saw Winfield was very close to the infield, Thomas knew the strong-armed outfielder would not need him for a relay throw. So Thomas ducked and spun around to watch the play at the plate.

Meanwhile, Winfield's throw came in hard, low, and right on target for the relay man. The ball hit Thomas directly on his backside, much like the Candiotti scenario.

After the game Winfield joked, "I finally hit the cutoff man."

A Not-So-Grand Slam

Cesar Cedeño of the Houston Astros hit what has to be one of the strangest hits, and perhaps the shortest grand slam, ever. It happened on September 2, 1971, when Cedeño hit a 200-foot fly ball with the bases loaded. Two Dodgers, second base-man Jim Lefebvre and right fielder Bill Buckner, converged on the ball.

They collided, and the ball fell in safely. By the time the Dodger defense could come up with the ball, it was too late. Cedeño had already circled the bases with a rather tainted grand slam.

More Inside-the-Park Wildness

On July 25, 1998, Turner Ward came to the plate as a pinch hitter for the Pittsburgh Pirates. He faced Dennis Martinez. What followed was about as bizarre as it gets. He hit the ball down off the plate, causing it to resemble a kid on a pogo stick, bouncing up the middle.

Atlanta Braves second baseman Tony Graffanino got to the ball, but he was only able to get a glove on it. That caused the ball to change directions, caroming past center-fielder Andruw Jones. Reportedly, Jones didn't hustle after the ball when it got by him, and Ward waltzed home with a strange inside-the-park homer.

Jeter Approves

The 1996 American League Rookie of the Year, Derek Jeter, was asked what trick plays he's seen that were interesting or unusual. Without skipping a beat, the Yankee shortstop responded, "Tony LaRussa batting the pitcher eighth over there in St. Louis—that's a little different!"

Arguments aside about whether or not this is actually a trick play, he's right. On July 9, 1998, when he penciled his starter in at the number-eight spot, LaRussa made Todd Stottlemyre the first big league pitcher in twenty years to bat anywhere but last in the order. Although Stottlemyre did hit .236 the previous season, there was another reason for the strategy. At first, some fans thought LaRussa was doing this because the man who did bat ninth, Placido Polanco, might be a weak hitter. Also, Polanco was making just his second major league start.

Fans and writers recalled that the last pitcher to hit higher than ninth was Philadelphia's Steve Carlton on June 1, 1979. In that case, it was true that Carlton was often a bigger threat with the bat than, say, Bud Harrelson, who hit ninth when Carlton was in the number-eight spot.

After much speculation, the truth came out. LaRussa revealed that his motive for the move was to get more men on base ahead of the heart of the lineup. Not a bad thought, especially when the aorta of that heart is big Mark McGwire, who was in the midst of chasing Roger Maris and the single-season home run record of 61.

Said the St. Louis manager, "I don't see how it doesn't make sense for the ninth-place hitter to be a legitimate hitter. This gives us a better shot to score runs. It's an extra guy on base in front of Ray Lankford, Mark McGwire, and Brian Jordan. The more guys who are on base, the less they'll be able to pitch around Mark."

LaRussa said he first conceived of the scheme at the All-

Star break and that it "doesn't have anything to do with the pitcher." Nothing, that is, except get his weak bat out of the way and allow a real hitter in the ninth spot to become, in effect, an additional leadoff hitter in front of McGwire and Company.

A logical question for LaRussa, then, was why not just drop McGwire to the cleanup position so he could always have three bona fide hitters preceding him. However, LaRussa said that because McGwire hits third, he comes to the plate in the 1st inning of every game, a big advantage in LaRussa's book.

Larry Lajoie's 1901 Batting Average Zooms from .401 to .422

Larry Lajoie, the great fielding, hard-hitting second baseman who played in the majors for 21 years (from 1896 through 1916), won the American League batting crown in 1901 with a purported .401 average while with the Philadelphia Athletics.

Of course, a .401 average for a full season is super, but in reality Lajoie did even better. Some 50-odd years later statisticians, led by the eagle-eyed Cliff Kachline, discovered that through mistakes in addition, Lajoie was short-changed by nine hits. He actually piled up 229 base hits, including 48 doubles, 13 triples, and a league-leading 14 homers, and that boosted his average by 21 points, from .401 to .422. That .422 still stands as the highest seasonal average by an American Leaguer. (Ty Cobb's .420 in 1911 and George Sisler's .420 in 1922 now rank second.)

After the conclusion of the 1901 season, league statisticians just didn't add up Lajoie's hit total correctly—his at bats remained the same at 543, and the nine additional base hits raised his lifetime big league average by one point, from .338 to .339.

The Strange Relationship between Walter Johnson and Ty Cobb

Walter Johnson versus Ty Cobb constituted perhaps the greatest and most ferocious pitcher/batter rivalry in the history of baseball. Their careers almost totally paralleled each other's. Johnson was active from 1907 through 1927, while Cobb was active from 1905 through 1928. (Cobb spent his first 22 years with the Detroit Tigers and then played his final 2 years in the majors with Connie Mack's Philadelphia Athletics.)

Thus, these two great players confronted each other for 21 years, 1907–1927. In his first time at bat against Johnson in a 1907 game pitting the Tigers against the Senators, Cobb hit a drag bunt and beat it out for a single.

In those 21 years, Cobb faced Johnson in some 400-plus total at bats and averaged .370—three points better than his record .367 lifetime mark. Cobb knew that Johnson would never pitch him inside, and thus was able to "dig in" at the plate.

Both men respected each other. In fact, they became good friends and kept in contact once their playing days were over.

Cobb's records are under constant review, especially by members of Society for American Baseball Research stats committee. His base-hit total is usually given at 4191. When Pete Rose challenged that mark during the 1985 season, reports floated around that Cobb actually pilled up 4192 base hits. At this moment, Cobb is being credited by SABR with only 4189. As Al Capp used to say in his famed *Li'l Abner* comic strip, "This is confoozin' but not amoozin'."

Was Cap Anson the First 3000-Hit Man?

Adrian C. "Cap" Anson, who played for the Chicago Cubs (originally known as the White Stockings) of the National League for 22 seasons, between 1876 and 1897, is generally considered to be the greatest all-around baseball star of the 19th century.

While Anson played all the positions in the game, including pitcher and catcher, he was primarily a first baseman. Most record books of the past have credited Anson with being the first major leaguer to rack up 3000 base hits. The hit total came to 3081 in 9084 official times at bat for an average of .339.

However, that hit figure is being seriously disputed, especially by John Thorn, who arguably ranks as the supreme authority on baseball as it was played in the 19th century. Thorn, a longtime committee chairman at SABR and the editor of *Total Baseball* (Warner Communications), maintains that Anson's hit total is actually 2995. Why the discrepancy? Thorn said, "There was a Chicago scorekeeper who was a red-hot Anson fan and, to guarantee Anson's batting championship, he would occasionally add a base hit here and there—hits that Anson never earned. Those 'gift' base hits added up to 86, according to my research."

Anson, nevertheless, was a towering figure in 19th-century baseball. He began his baseball career as an 18 year old with Marshalltown, Iowa—an independent league—in 1870, and then played for five seasons in the National Association, a professional circuit that was a direct predecessor of the National League, organized in 1876 as the first true major league. In the National Association he played his first year, in 1871, with Rockford, Illinois. In the next 4 seasons he starred with the Athletics of Philadelphia.

A true leader, he managed the Chicago Cubs/White Stockings from 1879 through 1897, and then served as a non-playing manager for the New York Giants in 1898.

In his 19 years as manager of Chicago, Anson led his team to 15 first-division finishes, including five pennants. "Big Anse," as Anson was also known, was elected to the Baseball Hall of Fame in 1939.

Even so, baseball stat fanatics are still trying to determine whether or not Cap Anson was a 3000-hit guy. As far as I'm concerned, I just throw up my hands as to the inexactitude of baseball records.

Albert Belle, 'The Silent'

Albert Belle, the controversial slugger, played his first 9 years in the major leagues with the Cleveland Indians, from 1988 through 1996, before he went to the Chicago White Sox as a free agent in 1997. In his tenure with the Indians, he established a team record by slamming 242 homers, and reached his absolute peak in 1995 when he became the first big leaguer to hit 52 doubles and 50 homers.

Unfortunately, Belle was noted as a surly character who didn't sign autographs for fans, refused to speak with reporters, and who on one occasion threw a baseball directly at a fan who was seated in the bleachers. The Indians ordered Belle to receive counseling. He seemed to improve his deportment for a time, but he kept slipping back to his old ways.

Despite his negative personality, Belle developed friendships with a number of coaches and teammates. On the Indians he was on particularly good terms with coach Dave Nelson and infielder Jim Thome.

In mid-September 1998, Belle revisited his old haunts at Cleveland's Jacobs Field with his Chicago White Sox. As Belle was awaiting his turn to take pregame batting practice, Dave Nelson came up to Belle, extended his hand, and said, "How ya doin', Albert?" Belle simply turned around, refused to shake hands, and never looked at Nelson. As Nelson walked back to the Indians dugout, Thome also came up to Belle for a friendly handshake. Again, Belle shunned the gesture and turned his back on Thome without looking at him. This may seem to be strange behavior, but as the old saying goes, "A leopard never changes his spots."

Mark McGwire, Home Run Hitter Extraordinare

During the 1998 season, Mark McGwire reached his peak as one of the premier home run hitters of all time, surpassing records established by such great sluggers of the past as Babe Ruth, Lou Gehrig, and Roger Maris.

Maris's record of 61 homers in '61 stood for 37 years until it was first broken by McGwire in 1998 and then by Sammy Sosa, outfielder with the Chicago Cubs, who also breached the Maris standard in the same '98 season. Sosa finished with 66 homers, but McGwire went on to virtually demolish the old mark when he concluded the season with an even 70 circuit clouts.

Even more incredibly, McGwire averaged 60 homers per season from 1996 to 1998—slamming a total of 180 balls out of the park. That is far and away a record. With Oakland in '96, McGwire led the National League with 52 homers, and then in '97 he hit 34 homers before being traded to the St. Louis Cards on July 31. For St. Louis, "Big Mac" homered 24 more times, giving him a total of 58. And his 70 in '98 gave him 180.

McGwire also became the first player in history to hit 50 or more homers in three consecutive seasons. Babe Ruth did hit 50 or more homers four times, but never for three seasons in succession.

Ruth's best 3-year total came during the 1926–1928 seasons when he slammed out 47, 60, and 54 homers, respectively for a total of 161. Many baseball historians felt that record would never be broken, but McGwire's three-season total bettered the Ruth mark by 19.

The big difference between the Ruth era and the McGwire era revolves around the fact that homers were not in vogue at the time the Babe was at his peak, from 1919 until the early 1930s. (During the first half-dozen years of his career with the Boston Red Sox, from 1914 to

1919, Ruth was almost primarily a pitcher—in 1919, he began to pitch sparingly, played the outfield almost every day, and hit 29 homers in 130 games.)

Ruth, in fact, on two separate occasions, in 1920 and 1927, personally hit more homers than each of the seven other teams in the American League. In 1920, the "Sultan of Swat" smacked out a record 54 homers and no team in the league matched that total.

In 1927, the Bambino, at the peak of his long ball power, whacked his then record 60 homers, and in that season no single American League team managed to top that total. Philadelphia "threatened" Ruth with 56 four-baggers.

In 1998, McGwire faced competition for the National League home run crown from Chicago's Sammy Sosa. McGwire and Sosa were tied at 66 going into the final weekend of the season. While Sosa did not connect for the circuit, McGwire hit four home runs in the last two games, giving him 70.

Because there were so few authentic home run hitters in the Ruth era, the Babe really stood out in the long ball department, but McGwire does his belting in a home-run-crazy period in baseball history.

Mark McGwire's Synthetically-Marked Home Run Balls

During the 1998 home-run race between St. Louis Cardinals' Mark McGwire and Chicago Cubs' Sammy Sosa, fans became obsessed with catching the home-run baseballs hit into the grandstands by that duo, especially by McGwire, who outpaced Sosa in the homer derby for most of the time.

From a historical perspective, Sal Durante, a New York fan, became a minor celebrity after he retrieved Roger Maris' 61st home run ball in the right field bleachers at Yankee Stadium on October 2, 1961. Durante reportedly sold the historic baseball for $5000.

National League officials were cognizant of the fact that any record-breaking McGwire homer baseball would undoubtedly be worth a lot of money on the open market. As the St. Louis slugger passed the 50-homer mark, every ball pitched to him was marked with synthetic DNA to make it identifiable. Thus, there would be no chance for anyone to pass off a "fake" McGwire home run ball.

On the last day of the 1998 season, on Sunday, September 27, at Busch Stadium in St. Louis, Mark McGwire, in his final time at bat, lined his 70th home run into a deep left field luxury-box suite. After a ferocious scramble, Philip Ozersky, a 26-year-old technician at the St. Louis University School of Medicine, came up with the ball.

Within 2 weeks after gaining possession of the ball, he received some four hundred inquires from dealers and collectors. Three St. Louis collectors got together and offered Ozersky a cool $1 million. Ozersky hired a lawyer to help him sort through all the offers.

The baseball is considered to be worth far more than $1 million, and now ranks as the single most valuable bit of baseball memorabilia.

One of the wackiest offers for the ball came from a man who identified himself as a distributor for a major American dollmaker. Ozersky's lawyer commented, "This guy thinks he can get a million threads out of the ball, insert one tiny thread into a million dolls, and sell them as Mark McGwire dolls with a piece of the ball in each one. That's not all. Then he wants to put the ball back together with [new] thread and sell it!"

Crazy Home Run Stats

Home runs were a relatively scarce commodity during the so-called Dead Ball Era, which ended in about 1919. In 1902, for example, the Philadelphia Phillies knocked only four balls out of the park, while the Pittsburgh Pirates led the National League with only nineteen! Tommy Leach of the Pirates (who completed the season with a fantastic 103–36 record to finish in first place, 27.5 games over second-place Brooklyn), was the "Home Run King" in that year with a puny total of 6. All told, the eight National League teams collectively hit 98 homers.

The pennant-winning Chicago White Sox of 1906, called "The Hitless Wonders," batted a sickly .228, the league's lowest mark ever by an A.L. pennant winner. The Sox hit a measly 6 homers all season, the lowest figure in the majors.

The White Sox, blessed with great pitching, whipped their crosstown rivals, the Cubs, in the World Series in 1906, although their team batting average fell below the "Mendoza line" at .198. But they still outhit the Cubs, who averaged .196.

The White Sox "outdid" themselves in the home run department in 1908 when they finished a strong third with an 88–64 mark, finishing below Cleveland and first-place Detroit. The Sox hit exactly three homers, the all-time low mark for any team in major league history. Team "leaders" in home runs for the Sox were Fielder Jones, Frank Isbell, and pitcher Ed Walsh, who each hit one round-tripper.

St. Louis and Boston led the team "home run parade" in 1908 with 21 each. Nowadays, guys like Sammy Sosa can hit that many homers in a month!

In the 1909 season, the White Sox (a fourth-place finisher at 78–74) really revved up the power department as the team hit a total of four homers—not terribly good, but one better than in 1908.

In 1945, the second-place Washington Senators (87–67; they finished only 1 game behind the pennant-winning Detroit Tigers) "led" the majors with the fewest home runs: 23. Incredibly enough, none of the homers was struck at the Senators' home park, the spacious Griffith Stadium. All came while the team was on the road. Harlond Clift paced the Washington homer "attack" with a total of eight.

The reasons for such low production? This was a World War II year, when baseballs were generally of poor quality and didn't travel well. Plus, Griffith Stadium's dimensions were onerous—the distance from home plate to the left field bleachers was an overwhelming 405 feet, and the distance down to the right field wall was a more modest 328 feet; the wall stood at an imposing 40 feet. What is really amazing is that no Senator hit an inside-the-park homer in that big ballpark. There are some things about baseball that cannot be explained!

Edd Roush's 48-Ounce Bat

Edd Roush (1893–1988), whose career spanned the 1913–1931 period and who was one of the greatest all-around players in the National League, was such a ferocious competitor that he became known as "The Ty Cobb of the National League." Roush gained Hall of Fame induction in 1962, with many baseball historians maintaining that he should have been given his bronze plaque at Cooperstown much earlier.

Roush's brilliant career was marked by one peculiarity: he used a 48-ounce bat, the heaviest bat ever used by a major league player. Contemporary players generally use bats weighing from 32 to 34 ounces, while a number, even sluggers, use 31-ouncers. The ballplayer of today feels he can gain greater bat speed with a lighter piece of lumber, enabling him to drive the baseball for a greater distance.

As Roush approached his 80th birthday, he said, "I hit very different from the way they hit today. I don't believe anyone used a bat heavier than the 48-ounce type I had. It was a shorter bat, with a big handle, and I tried to hit to all fields. Didn't swing my head off, just used a snap swing to make contact and drive the ball."

Roush retained his batting style and his 48-ounce wooden bat even though the lively ball came into being in 1919–1920 and other players went for much lighter clubs to generate more bat speed in order to hit for distance.

His tactics obviously paid off, because Edd Roush won two National League batting championships while with the Cincinnati Reds in 1917 and 1919, averaging .341 and .321, respectively. In a career total of 1,967 big league games, he averaged .323, and piled up 2,376 base hits. While he managed only 67 home runs, he hit 339 doubles and 183 triples, the latter being a very lofty stat.

Dave Kingman—Four Teams in One Season!

David Arthur Kingman, a 6-foot–6-inch, 220-pound home run slugger, slammed out 442 circuit blasts during his checkered 16-year big league career (1971–1986), and that gives him the distinction of having the most homers for a player not in baseball's Hall of Fame.

Throughout his tenure in the big leagues, Kingman was noted for not speaking with reporters and being generally hostile to the press as a whole. Early on, after he reached the majors with the San Francisco Giants in 1971, he claimed he was badly misquoted after giving out a series of interviews. And because of his generally ornery personality, Kingman went from one team to another, playing for a total of seven teams in both major leagues.

He was signed out of the University of Southern California by the San Francisco Giants and debuted with the parent club late in the 1971 season. Just before the start of the 1975 campaign, Kingman was sold to the New York Mets. By that time he had worn out his welcome with the Giants.

Big Dave remained with the Mets for the entire 1976 season, and then in '77 he really hit the jackpot for changing teams. In that year he played for exactly four of them. He went to the San Diego Padres in a June 15 trade, then on September 6 he was sold on waivers to the California Angels. His tenure with the Angels lasted for exactly 9 days because on September 15 he was sold to the New York Yankees. Yes, he did remain with the Yanks for the remainder of the season—2 whole weeks. Baseball historians found that playing for four big league teams within a single season at least ties a record.

The Yankees had no interest in signing Dave for 1978, and so the big slugger signed with the Chicago Cubs, where he remained, remarkably enough, for three full seasons.

Though he was on the disabled list for nearly a month in '78, Dave still managed to hit 28 homers in 119 games. In '79, when many baseball experts said that Dave was nearing the end of the road, he surprised everybody by having a "career year" as he led the league with 48 homers and 115 runs batted in while averaging a solid .288—all career highs for him. Dave's fortune declined in 1980 as he went on the disabled list three times, but when he was on the diamond he did play well, batting .278 in 81 games with 18 homers.

The Cubs soured on Kingman for a variety of reasons, particularly because of one grisly incident. He took a strong dislike to one female Chicago baseball reporter and expressed his displeasure with her writing by placing an expired rodent in her handbag.

Dave went over to the New York Mets at the beginning of 1981, and though he was happy about getting back to his old club, he again spent a bit of time on the DL, and was also benched at various times for striking out too much. Though he averaged .221 in 100 games, he did manage to slam 22 homers. The Mets knew that Kingman was a big gate attraction, a real threat at the plate. Moreover, fans liked to see his 450- to 500-foot "homers" into the stands during batting practice.

"King Kong" Kingman tried mightily to mend his ways in '82, and he kept himself off the bench by showing 'sporadic' and game-winning bursts of power. While he averaged a skinny .204 (going 109 for 535 in 149 games), he led the league with 37 circuit blasts and drove in 99 runs. No other player has led the league in homers with that low an average. A free—and sometimes wild—swinger, Dave struck out a league-leading 156 times. Dick Young, then a baseball writer for the New York *Daily News*, and long one of Dave's severest critics, called him "King Kong Kingman, The Strikeout King."

Kingman went on to have a career worst season in '83 as

he "rode the pines" for long periods. He batted less than his weight, .198 in 100 games, and homered only 13 times.

He certainly wasn't ready to quit baseball at that point. After his release by the New York Mets, he signed with the Oakland Athletics in 1984, and remained with the A's for three full seasons, retaining his reputation as an authentic home run threat. In those 3 years he hit exactly 100 homers—35, 30, and 35, respectively. His 1984 stats were particularly good: he averaged a strong .268 and knocked in 118 runs. Kingman was miffed that he didn't make the American League All-Star team in 1984, although he did play in the 1976 and 1980 All-Star games.

After being released by the A's following the '86 season, Kingman still had visions of reaching the magic 500 home run mark, and tried making a comeback in July '87 by signing with Phoenix of the Triple A Pacific Coast League. But after 20 games, with a sub-standard .203 average and only 2 homers, Dave hung up his uniform for good.

There are still those baseball writers who are long ball aficionados who feel Kingman is Hall of Fame material, despite his .236 lifetime batting average in the majors. They also point to his 1210 runs batted in and his home run ration of 6.6% (measured against official times at bat)—a stat good enough to give him a fifth-place spot on the all-time list among retired players. Dave's detractors point to his 1816 strikeouts—another fifth-place all-time rating.

We had the opportunity to interview Dave Kingman in October 1998. Frankly, we've never encountered a more affable and approachable interviewee. Said Kingman, "I may not have liked sportswriters when I was playing, and though I may have been a bit tough to get along with, I've always felt I was a decent person. Maybe I got a less than excellent reputation early in my career, but I was young, maybe a bit immature, but I have grown up. Remember, there are real pressures in playing big league baseball. Some basically excellent players fold because they cannot handle the pressure and play at their best before big and noisy crowds. I've felt that most baseball fans are fair and decent to the players, but the noisy boo-birds can get under your skin and warp your personality. By the same token, baseball writers in general are decent guys, but there are those who rip you all the time, and that kind of stuff can affect you. In general, I had a good career and have no regrets. Playing big league baseball is a rough-and-tumble profession."

Average Life of a Major League Baseball Is Only Six Pitches!

During major league baseball's so-called Stone Age, the late 1870s up to the turn of the century, a ball stayed in the game until it became so discolored, or even misshapen, that it had to be thrown out for a replacement. There are even confirmed reports that a single baseball was used for an entire game back in those old days! In fact, the use of beat-up balls continued to be a practice in the big leagues up to around the World War I period.

Edd Roush, a National League outfielder, heavy hitter, and Hall of Famer, often spoke of mashed-up baseballs being used in championship games. He spoke of this in great detail in an interview that appeared in Lawrence S. Ritter's landmark book *The Glory of Their Times*, published in 1966.

Roush, who played in the majors from 1913 to 1931, mostly with the Cincinnati Reds and New York Giants, recalled, "Until 1919, they had a dead ball. Well, the only way you could get a home run was if the outfielder tripped and fell down. The ball wasn't wrapped tight and lots of times it'd get mashed on one side.

"I've caught many a ball in the outfield that was mashed flat on one side. Come bouncing out there like a jumping bean. They wouldn't throw it out of the game, though. Only used about three or four balls in a whole game. Now they use 60 or 70."

Roush had that just about right. A recent study by Major League Baseball indicates that the average ball has a life of only about six pitches in a game. Rawlings Sporting Goods, Inc., based in Saint Louis, supplies all the baseballs used by the thirty teams making up the American and National Leagues. Those thirty teams gobble up 720,000 baseballs every season, according to Rawlings. A baseball retails for $6, but the major leagues buy them up at wholesale prices.

Mark McGwire, the St. Louis Cardinals slugger, hits a lot of homers out of the park, but even if he connects 60 or 70 times in a season, that will amount to only a fraction of the baseballs lost in action. And that says nothing of the many baseballs McGwire hits out of the park in batting practice. McGwire, in fact, draws crowds of fans who want to see him blast baseballs into the bleachers and over the stands in batting practice.

Rawlings Sporting Goods also supplies baseballs to most of the minor league teams, as well as to thousands of amateur teams scattered across the United States. Virtually all of the Rawlings baseballs are made overseas, particularly in Haiti, where the company takes advantage of low-priced labor. Baseball manufacture is labor intensive because the balls must be hand-stitched. Neither Rawlings nor any other company has been able to develop machinery to stitch baseballs on an assembly-line. The work must be done by human hands.

Rogers Hornsby Gets Sent Back to the 'Farm'

Rogers Hornsby, considered by most baseball historians as the greatest right-handed hitter of all time, made his major league debut with the St. Louis Cardinals in 1915 as a skinny 19-year-old infielder. After failing to become a creditable batsman during a trial period, he was called in by manager Miller Huggins, who said, "Son, we're going to have to send you back down to the farm."

Hornsby was reported as saying, "Mr. Huggins, you don't have to send me down to a farm, because my father already owns a farm down in Texas."

Hornsby did get the message finally, and he came back up to the Cardinals for the next season. By the time he finished his active career in 1937, he recorded a lifetime batting average of .358, second only to Ty Cobb's astounding .367.

Known as "The Rajah," Hornsby won the National League batting championship seven times, and reached the peak of his career in the five seasons between 1921 and 1925 when he averaged a phenomenal .403. In that 5-year stretch he swatted over .400 three times: .401 in 1922, .424 in 1924, and .403 in 1925.

The .424 mark remains the highest batting average achieved by a 20th-century player. Strangely enough, The Rajah did not receive the Most Valuable Player award. That honor went to the Brooklyn Dodgers fireballing pitcher, Dazzy Vance, who chalked up a 28–6 record. St. Louis Cardinals owner Sam Breadon was so incensed that Hornsby was passed over that he telephoned the league office and screamed, "What the hell must my guy do to get the MVP, hit .500?"

Hornsby remained in the game in one capacity or another until his death on January 5, 1963. He spent the preceding year as batting coach for the newly-organized New York Mets.

He always maintained, "Being sent down to the farm usually does a young player a lot of good."

Babe Ruth's 'Called Shot' in the 1932 World Series

The third game of the 1932 World Series still stands as one of the most dramatic clashes in the long history of the Fall Classic. The October 1 game pitted the Chicago Cubs at Chicago's Wrigley Field against the New York Yankees. New York had already won the first two games of the Series played at Yankee Stadium. Babe Ruth smashed a three-run homer off Cubs starter Charlie Root in the first inning, and in the early going, teammate Lou Gehrig also homered.

In the top of the fifth inning, with the scored tied at 4–4, Ruth faced Root again. With a count of two balls and two strikes, Ruth then seemed to gesture toward the center field bleachers, as if to indicate that's where he planned to deposit Root's next pitch. Or was he merely pointing at Root? Or was he addressing the Cubs bench with an exaggerated gesture, since the Cubs bench jockeys were teasing Ruth unmercifully?

Whatever the message, Ruth delivered on Root's next pitch. He swung viciously, and the ball sailed like a rocket toward center field and over the bleacher wall. This titanic blast put the Yankees ahead, 5–4.

Lou Gehrig matched Ruth's two home runs by following with a drive into the right field bleachers. The back-to-back home runs in the fifth stood up as the margin of victory as the Yankees, after trading runs with the Cubs in the ninth, prevailed 7–5.

Gehrig, the on-deck hitter at the time, obviously thought that the Babe had indeed called his shot. He said, "What do you think of the nerve of that big lug calling his shot and getting away with it?"

Charlie Root, on the other hand, strongly felt that Ruth never pointed to deep center field before the home run pitch. He said soon after the action was over, "If he had pointed to the home run landing spot, I would have knocked him down with the next pitch."

Babe Ruth himself was content to go along with the called-shot scenario, although he never really expounded upon the matter in any great detail.

In 1990, we had the opportunity to interview Billy Herman, who was the Cubs second baseman in the historic game. When we asked about Ruth's "called shot," Herman exclaimed without a moment's hesitation, "I never believed that the Babe called his shot. I was standing at second base, maybe 120 feet away from the batter's box, and though Ruth was gesticulating all over the place, I really don't think that any of his actions indicated that he would blast the ball over the center field bleachers. Still, the legend that the Babe did call the shot grew and grew. We'll never really know what was [on] Ruth's mind."

There's no question, however, that Game 3 broke the Cubs' spirit as the Yankees went on to win Game 4 by a 13–6 count, giving the Bronx Bombers a Series sweep. Now, more than two generations after that October 1, 1932, clash between the Yankees and Cubs, the legend continues to live on. Ruth's homer off Charlie Root remains unquestionably the greatest moment of his illustrious career and the most storied circuit blast in the entire history of the World Series. Babe Ruth played his final game in the major leagues over six decades ago, but the glory of his achievement will live on forever.

George 'Shotgun' Shuba: 'I'd Settle for the Licensing Fee'

George "Shotgun" Shuba, who played for the Brooklyn Dodgers from 1948 to 1955 and was the first National Leaguer to hit a pinch-hit homer in the World Series (in the '53 Series against the New York Yankees), discussed baseball salaries at length at a New York City card show. He said, "When I played, there were very few fringe benefits. Sure, some of the big stars like Stan Musial, Yogi Berra, Ted Williams, Joe DiMaggio, and Bob Feller made pretty fair money from commercial endorsements, but for the average player there weren't all that many opportunities to make money on the side. If I had the chance [now], I'd like to get a coaching job for a big league team, and I'd work for free. I'd just settle for the licensing fee."

The Major League Players Association has an agreement with Major League Baseball to share all licensing fees for the use of the MLB logo as well as individual team logos on commercial products. The royalty fee is currently pegged at about 8%. Thus, if a manufacturer retails a jacket bearing the MLB logo, or a team logo, for $50, the MLB Players' pool will receive $4. Tens of millions of dollars of income are generated this way.

Currently, each major league player, manager, and coach receives well over $100,000 in licensing fees annually. No wonder Shotgun Shuba would be willing to coach for zero salary!

Q&A

At Bat or Not at Bat?

Is it possible to get an official at bat without actually getting to bat?

Answer: Yes, it is. Rafael Ramirez of the 1989 Astros will attest to that. Houston manager Art Howe changed his usual batting order before the game one lazy summer afternoon. He switched Ramirez and Alex Trevino, but the respective players were unaware of the change in the line-up before the game began.

Trevino came to bat in Ramirez's scheduled spot and proceeded to get a base hit. But before the first pitch to Kevin Bass, the next hitter, the opposing team appealed, saying that Trevino had batted out of turn.

First, the umpires ruled that it was a double play. They called Trevino out for batting out of turn, and they also called Bass out. After Howe argued the call, however, the umpires correctly changed their ruling. They said that Ramirez, who was supposed to bat, was out, and they said that Bass, the next hitter in the order, was the proper batter.

Trevino's hit was taken away from him, but he was not charged with an at bat. Ramirez, on the other hand, never got an at bat, but he was charged with one.

The High Strike Zone

Pete Rose used to bat, and Rickey Henderson does today, out of an exaggerated crouch. Sometimes Henderson complains of high strike calls. Rose did, too. Why would umpires call a higher strike on Rose and Henderson than they would on other players?

Answer: Generally, the feeling among many umpires is that the exaggerated crouch was not in Rose's case and is not in Henderson's case their natural stance. Henderson, as Rose did, rises up out of the crouch as the moundsman delivers his pitch to the plate. Rule 2.00, Strike Zone—Umpires must use their judgment on such calls. If this is not the player's normal stance and it is being used for trickery, the umpire should call a strike if the pitch is in what he judges to be the batter's normal strike zone, that is, the space over the plate between the batter's armpit level and the top of his knees.

Who Gets the Putout?

The Padres have the bases loaded in a game against the Giants. Carmelo Martinez hits his first pitch to the fence in left field. The ball should be caught, but the left fielder for the Giants misplays the ball, it hits the base of the fence, and two runs score. But the Padre runner on first base, thinking that the ball would be caught, acts indecisively, and Martinez passes him on the base path between first and second.

Who is called out? Who gets the putout?

Answer: Martinez is called out by the umpire for passing the runner. Rule 7.08 h—The fielder nearest the play gets credit for the put out. If the passing of the runner occurred closer to second base than to first, the second baseman would get the putout; if the passing took place closer to first base than to second, the first baseman would get it. Rule 10.10 [b-4].

The situation occurred in County Stadium, Milwaukee, in 1986: The Brewers, who were hosting the Yankees, loaded the bases in the bottom of the first inning. Robin Yount was on third base, Cecil Cooper on second base, and Gorman Thomas on first base. Ernie Riles then hit a ball to the base of the wall. It should have been caught, but it was misplayed by the Yankee outfielder, and it bounced off the base of the wall. Two runs scored. But an indecisive Thomas was passed between first and second base by the hard-running Riles.

Riles was called out by the umpire. The putout went to Willie Randolph, the Yankee second baseman.

Sacrifice Fly?

The Mets are in Cincinnati for a mid-season game in 1986. They have Wally Backman on third base and Keith Hernandez on first base with no outs. Darryl Strawberry hits a slicing fly ball to the Reds left fielder. It is deep enough to score Backman from third base, but definitely a catchable ball. The fielder drops the ball, however, while Backman scores and Hernandez advances to second base on the play.

Does Strawberry get an RBI? Since the left fielder made an error on the play, is the sacrifice taken away from Strawberry, and does he get an at bat instead?

Answer: The official scorer gave Strawberry a sacrifice fly and RBI and didn't charge him with an at bat. The scorer reasoned that the hit, with less than two out, was far out enough to score Backman, whether the fielder had dropped the ball or not.

Game-Winning RBI?

In Game Seven of the 1962 World Series between the Yankees and the host Giants, New York's Ralph Terry outpitched San Francisco's Jack Sanford, 1-0. In the sixth inning of that game, the Yankees loaded the bases with no out, and then Tony Kubek drove home the only run of the game when he grounded into a double play.

Did Kubek receive credit for a game-winning RBI?

Answer: No. Rule 10.04 b—Do not credit a run batted in when the batter hits into a force double play or a reverse force double play. NOTE: There does not have to be a game-winning RBI in every game.

The Assisted Home Run

The Tigers are playing the Orioles in a July game. Detroit's Darrell Evans hits a long fly ball to left-center field. The Orioles center fielder drifts back with the ball and appears to catch it easily as he backs into the fence. Upon the player's contact with the fence, however, the ball pops out of his glove and bounces over the fence.

Is Evans' hit a double or a home run?

Answer: It's a home run. Rule 6.09 h.—The ball is considered to be "in flight." Any ball in flight that leaves the park in fair territory is ruled a home run. If it had bounded off any physical structure of the park, such as the fence, instead of a player's glove, before clearing the playing field fence, it would be ruled a double.

The above play also occurred in an actual game on July 24, 1986 in a contest between the White Sox and the Orioles. Greg Walker of the White Sox hit the ball. Freddie Lynn lost it. Home run.

The Hot Corner

One afternoon in the late 1940s, Joe DiMaggio hit a hard smash down the third-base line that caromed off the arm of Detroit third baseman George Kell into the stands behind the visitor's dugout.

How many bases was DiMaggio awarded?

Answer: Two. Rule 7.05 f—He gets the same number of bases he would have gotten if a fair ball he had hit went through or under, or stuck in, a fence, scoreboard, shrubbery, or vines.

Hit Batsman, not Walk

In a game between the Expos and the Reds, Montreal has Hubie Brooks on third base, two outs, and Andres Galarraga at the plate with a full count.

Tom Browning, the Cincinnati pitcher, hits Galarraga with the next pitch, and the ball rolls back to the screen. Before catcher Bo Diaz can retrieve the ball, Brooks scores and Galarraga hustles safely to second base.

Is Brooks allowed to score, and can Galarraga stretch out an extra base on the play?

Answer: No. Galarraga has been hit with a pitched ball. He has not walked. The ball is dead once it hits Galarraga and neither base runner can advance. Brooks is sent back to third base, Galarraga is returned to first base. Rule 5.09 a.

The Free Swinger

Gus Zernial of the Athletics was so strong that his teammates called him "Ozark Ike." One day an opposing pitcher bounced a two-strike curveball a foot in front of the plate. But Zernial was fooled by the pitch and swung at it. To almost everyone's surprise, however, he lifted the ball over the left-center field fence for a home run. It was no surprise that the opposition contended that the swing was illegal and Zernial should be a strikeout victim.

What's your interpretation?

Answer: It's a home run. Rule 2.00 A BALL—if the batter hits such a pitch, the ensuing action will be the same as if he had hit the ball in flight.

Follow-Up Scenario

Let's carry the preceding scenario a few steps further. Suppose (1) Zernial, with two strikes on him, did not swing and the ball bounced through the strike zone? Or (2) the ball bounced and struck Zernial? Or (3) Zernial swung and missed the bouncing ball?

Answer: One, it would be a ball. Two, Zernial would be awarded first base. Three, the catcher's simply fielding the ball cleanly would not constitute an out. The batter must be tagged as on any dropped third strike, or he must be thrown out at first base (unless first base is occupied before there are two outs.) Rule 2.00 A BALL and 6.05 c.

The Invisible Mark

Suppose a player such as Roger Maris or Henry Aaron is approaching a cherished home-run mark, and the record to be made is dependent on such a player hitting a ball over the fence and possibly into the stands. How can the respective leagues be assured that the ball being returned by the person who claims to possess it is authentic? After all, the ball will eventually end up in the Baseball Hall of Fame in Cooperstown, N.Y.

Answer: The respective leagues do it by using "Henry Aaron balls." When Aaron passed 700 career home runs, the umpires began to mark balls in games which Aaron played with invisible ink, and placed them in a special bag. When Aaron came to the plate to hit, those balls were used.

Every time he hit a home run in his countdown towards Babe Ruth's record, at least ten spectators would claim that they had the official ball. But only one of the balls that the claimants presented was authentic.

Lost Run

Almost everyone on occasion loses track of a run that is scored. But usually not the official scorer! In the following case, the official scorer did lose track of a run that scored. But there were extenuating circumstances.

In a 1989 contest between the host Yankees and the Brewers, New York was leading Milwaukee 4–1 in the bottom of the eighth inning. The Yankees had Mike Pagliarulo on third base and Bob Geren on first base with one out when manager Dallas Green flashed the suicide squeeze sign to batter Wayne Tolleson. The batter bunted the ball in the air to Brewer pitcher Jay Aldrich, who threw the ball to first base to double off Geren. In the meantime, Pagliarulo crossed home plate before the third out of the inning was recorded at first base.

In this situation could the Brewers have recorded a "legal fourth out?"

Answer: In order to do so, however, they would have had to make an appeal at third base before every infielder, including the pitcher, in walking off the field, had crossed the foul lines into foul territory. (Rule 7.10 d.) But they didn't do it. So even though Pagliarulo had left third base too soon—and he didn't return to the base to retouch it—his run counted because the double play was not a force or reverse force twin-killing.

At the time, umpire Larry Barnett didn't give an explicit explanation to the official scorer, so the run wasn't posted—until after the game! Thirty thousand fans left the park thinking that the final score was 4–1. Many of them found out in the next day's newspapers that the official score was 5–1, and that unknowingly they had witnessed one of the most unusual plays in the history of the game.

Umpire Barnett said after the game, "I've been in this game twenty-six years, and I've never seen that play."

Manager Green went seven years further: "I've been in this game thirty-three years, and I've never seen that play."

Loose Bat

Dave Winfield of the Angels has been known to let the bat slip out of his hands after a hard swing. Suppose, in a game against the White Sox, he hits a ball to shortstop Ozzie Guillen and lets go of the bat in the infielder's direction. While Guillen is trying to avoid the flying missile, the ball rolls past him for a "base hit."

Is it a case of safe hit or safety first?

Answer: Rule 6.05 h—If a whole bat is thrown into fair territory and interferes with the defensive player's attempt to make a play, interference shall be called, whether intentional or not. In this case, Winfield is out.

But, suppose Winfield broke his bat during contact with the ball, and the broken half of the bat hit Guillen, thereby preventing him from making the play.

Interference?

Rule 6.05 h—If a bat breaks and part of it is in fair territory, and it is hit by a batted ball or part of it hits a runner or fielder, play shall continue and no interference shall be called.

The Muffled-Ball Call

Mike Greenwell of the Boston Red Sox, with two out and no one on base, pops up to the Milwaukee first baseman, who first bobbles the ball and then loses it in fair territory. When he loses the ball, it hits Greenwell on the fly, in foul territory, and then bounces off him, without hitting the ground, into the glove of second baseman Jim Gantner, who is backing up the play. Is Greenwell the third out of the inning?

Answer: No. It is considered a fair ball, but no catch. The Brewer first baseman initially touched the ball over fair territory. Rule 2.00 A CATCH—It is not a catch if a fielder touches a fly ball which then hits a member of the offensive team or an umpire and is then caught by another defensive player.

Steps/Forward and Backwards

An Oakland A's slugger hits the ball over the left-field fence, but in rounding the bases, he misses touching first base. En route to home plate, between second and third base, the first-base coach attracts his attention to the fact that he missed first base, and encourages him to return to touch the missed bag.

The batter-runner retouches second base, returns to and tags first base, and then continues his home-run trot around the bases.

Is this legal?

Answer: No. The ball is dead when it leaves the park. When the ball is dead, a runner may not return to touch a missed base after he has touched the next base. When the ball becomes live, the defensive team should appeal the play. If the defensive team doesn't appeal the play, the run counts. Rule 7.02, 7.10 b, APPROVED RULING, 7.10 b, PLAY b.

The Suspended Speaker

The Minnesota Twins are losing by three runs in the bottom of the ninth inning when Kent Hrbek hits what appears to be a game-winning grand-slam home run. But the ball hits a speaker that is suspended from the ceiling of the Hubert H. Humphrey Metrodome, and it comes down in fair territory, where it is caught by Boston Red Sox right fielder Dwight Evans.

Is the hit an out, a ground-rule double, or a home run?

Answer: It is an out! Situations such as this one are governed by the home team's ground rules. A ball that hits either the roof or a speaker in fair territory at the Metrodome is in play. If the fielder catches the ball on the fly, the batter is out and the runners advance at their own risk.

Four-Run Mistake

The White Sox have Carlton Fisk on third base, Don Pasqua on second base, and their designated-hitter on first base when Ozzie Guillen, with two out, hits an inside-the-park home run. The runner on first base misses touching second base, however, and the second baseman, upon completion of the play, calls for the ball, touches second and appeals the play.

How many runs count?

Answer: None. Rule 4.09a, 7.08 e, and 10.06 b—The appeal becomes a simple force play. It nullifies all four runs. Also, a batter does not get a hit on a play that results in a force play. Guillen is charged with an at bat, but no hit is credited.

Holding His Bat High

Orlando Cepeda, of the Giants and four other major-league teams, believed each bat had only one hit in it, so as soon as he got a hit with a bat, he would discard it.

Other players tend to be overly protective of their bats. They use pine tar on them, they hone them, and they bone them. One such player carried his protective attitude to an extreme a few years back. He hit a triple and carried his bat with him, sliding into third base with his bat held high in his right hand. He did this for two reasons: one, he didn't want his bat to pick up a spot when he dropped it, and two, he didn't want another player to use it.

But is it legal for a player to hold onto his bat while he's running out his hit?

Answer: The batter-runner in this instance is certainly eccentric, but his eccentricity is a legal act. Rule 9.01 c— There is no rule which prohibits the batter-runner from carrying a bat while running the bases, so long as it does not hinder, confuse, or impede the defense.

The Three-Base Foul Ball

Is it possible for a batter to get three bases on a foul ball?

Answer: Yes, it is. Rule 2.00 FAIR BALL. Consider the following situation: The White Sox batter dribbles a ball down the third-base line. The Red Sox catcher runs down the line, throws his glove at the ball, and hits it. A ball is not fair or foul until it passes first or third base or it settles in foul territory. If a fielder throws his glove at a ball and hits it, the batter is awarded three bases.

Frank Howard once hit a *bunt triple*—on the fair side of the third-base line. The opposing third baseman was playing "Hondo" as usual, five feet out on the outfield grass. The pitcher came over and almost fielded the ball, but it just got by him. In a state of frustration, he threw his glove at the rolling ball—and hit it. That's an automatic triple—one of the shortest in the history of the game!

Two-Strike Bunt Foul

Tony Gwynn of the Padres is on first base, and he is off and running with the pitch when pitcher Ed Whitson bunts a two-strike pitch into the air and foul down the third-base line. Kevin Mitchell, the third baseman for the Giants, sees that the pop-up is a catchable ball.

Should he catch it or should he let it drop to the ground?

Answer: He should catch the ball and double Gwynn off first base. Whitson, of course, is a strikeout victim as the result of having bunted foul with two strikes on him (Rule 7.08 d), but when a two-strike foul bunt is caught, the ball remains in play—just as on any other legal catch. The runner, therefore, can be retired before he retouches first base.

Triple Play?

The Royals have the bases loaded with no out when the batter, with an oh-two count on him, decides to surprise the defense by dragging a bunt. However, he pops the ball up halfway to the mound.

The runners think that the pop-up is an Infield Fly, so they can't remain close to their respective bases. But the pitcher can't reach the ball, and the backspin on it brings it back to the catcher, who is standing on home plate. He picks the ball up, with his foot on the plate, and throws it to the third baseman, who fires it to the second baseman for an apparent triple play.

Is it?

Answer: Yes. Rule 2.00, Infield Fly and 7.08 e—An attempted bunt cannot be an Infield Fly.

The Defense Appeals

The Blue Jays have the bases loaded, two out, and a three-two count on the batter. The pay-off pitch by the Seattle Mariner hurler goes wild, and the ball rolls back to the screen. The catcher, retrieving the ball, fires it into left field in an attempt to throw out the runner at third base. All three runners score and the batter-runner trots safely into second base. Then the first baseman appeals that the batter-runner missed touching first base. The umpire upholds the appeal. Do the runs count?

Answer: No. The runs don't count because the third out of the inning was made on the batter-runner at first base. Rule 4.09 a and 7.04 d—NOTE.

Interference at the Plate

Mark McGwire of the Oakland A's is the batter, Rick Cerone, who likes to position himself close to the batter, is the catcher for the Boston Red Sox. McGwire takes a mighty cut at a Dennis "Oil Can" Boyd fastball, and hits the ball over the left-field fence for an apparent home run. But the home-plate umpire notices that McGwire's bat made contact with Cerone's glove before it connected with Boyd's pitch.

Does McGwire get only one base because of Cerone's interference, or does he get four bases?

Answer: Four bases. Rule 6.08 c—The batter becomes a runner and is entitled to four bases when the catcher or any other fielder interferes with him. If a play follows the interference, the manager of the team at bat may tell the plate umpire that he elects to decline the interference penalty and accept the play.

To Be or Not to Be

A Milwaukee Brewer manager of recent years sent up a pinch-hitter in the sixth inning, then changed his mind when the player got into the batter's box and replaced him with another pinch-hitter.

Later in the game he sent up to the plate the pinch-hitter he had replaced to substitute-swing again.

Could he do that?

Answer: No, he couldn't. Even if the initial pinch-hitter was not announced the first time, he was considered to be in the game when he took his position in the batter's box. Rule 3.08 (a-2).

Two-Run Triple?

The Twins have Kirby Puckett at third base, a runner at first base, and Gary Gaetti at bat with two out.

As the pitcher begins his wind-up, the umpire calls a balk, but the hurler releases the ball, and Gaetti hits a two-run triple. The second baseman notices, however, that the runner from first base missed touching second base, and he appeals the play. The umpire agrees and calls the runner out.

Does Puckett's run count?

Answer: No. Rule 8.05 PENALTY, APPROVED RULING—The balk was nullified when the batter hit safely and the two runners advanced at least one base. In this case, the runner who missed second base is nevertheless recognized to have advanced to second base. Also, the third out was made on a force play, so no runs score.

On the Rebound

Jack Clark of the Padres smashes a line drive that hits the pitcher's rubber and rebounds toward home plate. Catcher Gary Carter of the Mets reaches over the plate into fair territory, catches the ball, and throws it to first baseman Keith Hernandez for the out.

Or is it a foul ball?

Answer: Clark is out. Carter fielded the ball in fair territory, so the ball is in play. If he had fielded the ball in foul territory, it would have been a foul ball. Rule 2.00, A FAIR BALL—It is not the position of the catcher's feet or body that counts, but the position of the ball when it is touched.

No Grand Slam?

Rob Deer of the Milwaukee Brewers comes to the plate in the fifth inning with the bases loaded and two out. He hits a grand-slam home run over the left-center-field fence, but the runner who was on first base misses second base and is subsequently called out on appeal.

How many runs score? What kind of a hit does Deer get awarded?

Answer: No runs score and Deer does not get credited with a hit. Rule 7.12—If, upon appeal, the preceding runner is the third out, no runners following him shall score. If such third out is the result of a force play, neither preceding nor following runners shall score.

Unannounced Pinch Hitter

Suppose a manager sends up a long-ball threat as a pinch-hitter in the bottom of the ninth inning of a tie game, and fails to notify the home-plate umpire of the substitution. Then the batter hits the first pitch over the fence for the apparent game-winning home run. But the opposing manager appeals the pinch-hit, saying that the substitute batted out of order since he never officially entered the game.

Is it a proper appeal?

Answer: No. The game is over as the result of the home run. The batter did not hit out of order because he was already a substitute. Batting out of order occurs when a player already in the game bats in the improper spot. Rule 3.08 a-2—If no announcement of a substitute is made, the substitute shall be considered as having entered the game when, if a batter, he takes his place in the batter's box.

Consecutive Game Streak

On the night that Pete Rose's hitting streak of 44 consecutive games was broken, he went hitless in four official at bats against Atlanta Braves pitchers Larry McWilliams and Gene Garber. Suppose he had gone to the plate five official times that evening and had walked, reached first base on catcher's interference, sacrifice-bunted, hit a sacrifice fly, and been hit by a pitch.

Would his streak have remained intact? Why? Why not?

Answer: Rose's streak would have ended. Rule 10.24 b—The streak shall terminate if the player has a sacrifice fly and no hit. A consecutive-game hitting streak shall not be terminated if all the player's plate appearances—one or more—result in a base on balls, hit batsman, defensive interference, or sacrifice bunt.

Batter's Request

In the bottom of the seventh inning, the Twins have Kent Hrbek on third base with two out. The batter, with an oh-two count, steps out of the batter's box while White Sox pitcher Britt Burns is delivering the next pitch. He does not request time out. Burns stops in the middle of his delivery. The umpire makes no call.

What is the call?

Answer: No call. Rule 6.02 b—The batter shall not leave his position in the batter's box after the pitcher comes to Set Position, or starts his wind-up. If the pitcher pitches, the umpire shall call "Ball" or "Strike," as the case may be. If, after the pitcher starts his wind-up or comes to a "set position" with a runner on, he does not go through with the pitch because the batter has stepped out of the box, it shall not be called a balk. Both the batter and the pitcher have violated a rule, and the umpire shall call time, and both the batter and pitcher start over from scratch.

Where Do You Bat Him?

Imagine you're at the helm of a pennant-winning team, and you're about to play the fourth game of the World Series. Would you consider batting your starting pitcher somewhere other than the traditional number-nine slot in the lineup?

Answer: You might, if the pitcher were George Herman Ruth. Babe Ruth left the ranks of pitchers after 1919, although he did pitch in five scattered contests after that. He became a pretty fair hitter, with a .342 lifetime batting average and 714 homers.

Actually, he was a fine hitter even while pitching—why do you suppose his manager moved him to the outfield full-time? In the last two seasons in which he spent a significant time on the mound (1918 and 1919) he was used as an outfielder in 59 and 111 games respectively. He hit 11 homers in 1918, then 29 the following year. Both totals were good enough to lead the American League. He also drove in 66 runs, followed by 114 runs.

So, with all that in mind, it's not so shocking to learn that in 1918 (his 11-homer year), in his final Series outing as a pitcher, he hit in the sixth spot for the Boston Red Sox. This marked the only time in World Series history that a starting hurler appeared any place but ninth in the batting order.

Aaron and His 756 Homers

Every good fan knows Hank Aaron is the all-time home run king, with 755 career blasts. But here's a situation involving Aaron and home runs that many fans don't recall:

Back on August 18, 1965, in St. Louis, Aaron faced Cards pitcher Curt Simmons. Simmons lobbed a blooper pitch to Hammerin' Hank. The superstar right fielder slashed the ball on top of the pavilion roof at Sportsman's Park for a tape-measure blow. As Aaron stepped into the pitch, he actually wound up making contact with the ball while one foot was entirely out of the batter's box. Does this matter? Was Aaron permitted to trot around the bags with a home run, was it a "no pitch" call, or was he ruled out?

Answer: When a batter makes contact with a pitch while outside the box, he is declared out. Aaron would own 756 homers if it weren't for the sharp eyes of home plate ump Chris Pelekoudas.

Oldies but Goodies

Let's say you are umping a game back in 1919, and the batter is none other than the Sultan of Swat, Babe Ruth. He drills a ball that flies by the foul pole in fair territory, then wraps around the pole before smacking into a seat in foul grounds. What's your call here—home run or merely a long, harmless foul ball?

Answer: This is a trick question. Today the ball is ruled fair. However, prior to 1920, such a play was called foul. The umpires judged the ball fair or foul by where it landed. Unlike Aaron and his "lost" home run, Babe Ruth didn't, in reality, lose any home runs because of this rule, but obviously some men did back then.

Penalty for Suffering Pain?

Mo Vaughn is known for crowding home plate. He even wears a special protective device on his right arm. What would happen if the big first baseman were hit by a pitch on an 0–2 delivery as he was swinging at the ball?

Answer: It's a strikeout, and any runners on base must freeze. The ball is dead, so they can't advance.

Another Hit-by-Pitch Scenario

Must a batter make a legitimate effort to avoid getting hit by the ball, or is the fact that he was hit sufficient to earn a free trip to first base?

Answer: The batter must try to dodge the pitch. Perhaps the most famous case involving this rule occurred in 1968. Don Drysdale, Los Angeles's standout right-hander, was in the midst of a fantastic streak of shutout innings.

In a game versus the Giants, he faced a bases-loaded, no-out situation. Dick Dietz, the San Francisco catcher, was at the plate with a two-and-two count. Drysdale came in tight with a pitch that hit him. Dietz got ready to stroll to first base, forcing in a run.

But wait a minute—home plate umpire Harry Wendelstedt ruled that Dietz had made no move to avoid the pitch. Despite an argument that raged on and on, the ruling stood, and the pitch was ball three.

When Dietz proceeded to fly out, Drysdale's shutout streak continued, eventually stretching to 58 2/3 innings. Incidentally, that record was later broken by another Dodger, Orel Hershiser.

More Delays

Albert Belle, Baltimore's volatile slugger, is at the plate. Let's say he gets irate over a strike call you, the umpire, just made. He starts to jaw with you. After a few moments, you get fed up with the delay and tell Belle to get in the box and quit squawking. What do you do if Belle refuses to obey your orders?

In this case, you would order the man on the mound to pitch the ball. As a punishment, you would call that pitch a strike even if it isn't in the strike zone. In addition, if the batter still refuses to step in and face the pitcher, every subsequent pitch is ruled a strike until the recalcitrant batter whiffs.

In real life, this happened to Frank Robinson after he argued about a called strike two. Moments later, the umpire called strike three, and the future Hall-of-Famer had lost the battle, and the war.

Potent Lineup

Has a team ever had as many as six players in the lineup drive in 100 or more runs during a season?

Answer: No, but the 1936 Yankees featured an incredibly productive lineup with a record five men who had more than 100 ribbies.

The men included three future Hall-of-Famers: first base-man Lou Gehrig, who amassed 152 RBI; center fielder Joe DiMaggio, who added 125; and catcher Bill Dickey with his 107 RBI. In addition, Tony Lazzeri had 109, and George Selkirk contributed 107.

Fanning Infrequently

Has a major-leaguer gone an entire season while striking out fewer than, say, 25 times?

Answer: Not in a long time, but yes, it has been done. In fact, Cleveland's Joe Sewell did this with ease. Sewell was known for his bat control, and, in 1925 and 1929, he truly showcased that talent. During those seasons, he struck out a mere eight times, four each year. Men have been known to strike out four times in a day; it took an entire year for Sewell to do that. Furthermore, he had 608 at bats in 1925 and 578 in 1929.

Impotent Bats

Has there ever been a season in which nobody in the entire American League hit .300 or better? Could such a season of pitchers' domination occur?

Answer: Although there was never a season without at least one .300 hitter, there was a year in which only one man topped that level. The year 1968 was known as the Year of the Pitcher. That season, the American League batting title went to Boston's Carl Yastrzemski, who hit .301. The next-best average was a paltry .290. The A.L. pitchers prevailed that year; five of them had ERAs under 2.00.

That was also the season that one of every 5 games resulted in a shutout. It seemed as if every time St. Louis Cardinal Bob Gibson pitched, he tossed a shutout (he had 13). His ERA (1.12) was the fourth lowest in baseball history. Finally, that season also featured the game's last 30-game winner, Detroit's Denny McLain (31–6).

You vs. LaRussa

After using Polanco in the ninth position in the batting order, LaRussa had the freedom to use other personnel. For example, in the next two games, he hit catcher Tom Pagnozzi ninth. Later, he used Pat Kelly at second base instead of Polanco, and hit Kelly ninth as well.

For your data bank, Pagnozzi entered 1998 with a lifetime batting average of .255. He had collected 43 home runs and had driven in 310 runs over 876 big league games. As a catcher, you'd expect him to be a slow runner. At best, he probably ranks as an average runner.

Would he be much help if he got on base, or would he clog up the base paths? Would the next three batters benefit when he got on base, or would there simply be more double plays? Would it be smarter to go with a faster man, such as Kelly?

Answer: While LaRussa didn't stick with Pagnozzi for long (using a variety of players instead), this pitcher-batting-eighth strategy doesn't offer a simple answer. In a way, the jury is still out because although the ex-periment seems to have failed, other managers might employ this tactic in the future. Who knows? You're on your own for this call.

One thing is for sure: LaRussa felt he had to do something to help his slugger. By July 28, McGwire led the majors in intentional walks drawn with 22. That was more than twice as many intentional walks as the American League leader, Ken Griffey, Jr., who had 10.

Further, Big Mac had been walked a total of 102 times (and ended with a league-record 162 bases on balls). In 1961, when Maris set the home run record, he drew just 94 walks because he had better protection around him in the Yankees' batting order. Pitchers that year were apparently more fearful of pitching to Mickey Mantle (126 walks, best in the majors). In 1998, nobody really wanted to pitch to McGwire, and the St. Louis offense wasn't exactly awe-inspiring.

Now it should also be noted that LaRussa did indeed scrap the McGwire experiment after using his unique lineup just once in spring training of 1999. In 1998, the Cardinals' record with that lineup in effect was 46–36, but LaRussa said it proved to be a distraction. He said he didn't think coaches and managers should be the focus in the media: "...the more they're in the paper, the worse it is. The game is about the players."

He also said the controversial lineup had only one failing: "The only time you get burned, according to somebody that wants to second-guess you, is when you've got the bases loaded and two outs and the eighth-place hitter comes up. Well, yeah, I'd rather have a position player than a pitcher bat there, but there's almost no other [negative] situation."

Well, according to a statistical study, LaRussa was wrong in undertaking this experimental batting order. Instead of giving McGwire more opportunities to drive in runs, "Big Mac" had fewer chances, losing about 20 runs driven in. Thus, the experiment may have cost him the RBI crown in 1998 (he wound up 11 behind leader Sammy Sosa).

By the way, around the time the experiment began, LaRussa said he felt McGwire would break the Maris record in 1998, "if they [opposing pitchers and managers] challenge him to the very end." They did, and he did—easily. Big Mac swatted number 62 on September 8!

As a side note, in 1998 Jack McKeon, manager of the Cincinnati Reds, stated that he had managed a team in the minors that hit a pitcher in the fifth position. The pitcher was Jackie Collum, and the team was the Triple-A Vancouver squad back in 1962. In McKeon's case, he batted the pitcher that high simply because the team's offense was so weak. McKeon said he even used Collum as his number-one pinch hitter.

To Squeeze or Not to Squeeze

Do managers squeeze with a lefty in the batter's box, or is that considered poor strategy?

Answer: It's not poor strategy. Wade Boggs said, "I think if they're a good bunter, it doesn't matter if they're left handed or right-handed. Kevin Stocker's a switch hitter and we've squeezed with him batting left-handed. If the runner does his part at third base and gets a late enough break so the pitcher doesn't dictate [the play], all you have to do is put the ball down, and the runner scores anyway."

Bobby Cox agrees, "We do it all the time with [southpaw pitcher] Tom Glavine. If you can get the bunt down, I know the catcher has a clear look at the runner and all that, but that doesn't make any difference. As long as the guy doesn't leave early, you're in good shape."

Quotations

When told his salary was more than the earnings of President Hoover, this man stated, "Oh, yeah? Well, I had a better year than he had."

—*Babe Ruth*

Who was the player Dante Bichette was referring to when he said: "He's the kid who, when he played Little League, all the parents called the president of the league and said, 'Get him out of there, I don't want him to hurt my son.' I had my mom call the National League office to see if she could do it for me."

—*Mark McGwire*

After hitting four homers in a game to tie the single-game record, this power hitter said quite correctly, "I had a good week today."

—*Bob Horner*

CHAPTER

The Pitcher's Mound

Wrong Pitcher

Once in a while a manager will signal to the bull pen for one pitcher, but a different one will show up at the mound.

And it can happen to the best. One day in the late 1950s Yankee manager Casey Stengel thought his starting pitcher, Whitey Ford, was getting tired, so he called the bull pen and asked for Johnny Kucks, a sinkerball pitcher, to come on in relief. But bull-pen catcher Darrell Johnson, who answered the phone, thought Stengel said "Trucks" instead of "Kucks."

When (Virgil) Trucks showed up at the mound, Stengel almost fainted, but he regained his composure and didn't say anything. Only Ford and catcher Yogi Berra knew that Stengel had wanted Kucks. As it turned out, Trucks threw one pitch, a game-ending double play ball, and then Stengel expounded to the reporters for hours after the game the reason he called on Trucks, rather than Kucks, in that crucial situation.

Only Ford and Berra knew that Casey really wanted Kucks.

Drysdale Humor

Umpire Augie Donatelli once raced out to the mound and searched Dodger pitcher Don Drysdale, whom he suspected of throwing a spitball. First he checked Drysdale's hat, glove, and uniform. Finally, he ran his fingers through Don's hair. When he was through with his futile search, Drysdale said, "Didn't you forget something?"

"What?" Donatelli asked.

"Usually when people run their fingers through my hair, they give me a kiss, too."

A Hot, Dry Day

Pitcher Jerry Reuss is a player who likes to have a few laughs around the ball park. At some one else's expense, of course.

For example, one day in Los Angeles the temperature was in the high nineties and Frank Pulli, the umpire who was working the plate, was desperately looking forward to a cold drink. Reuss, feeling sorry for Pulli, sent the ball boy out with a drink for the umpire in between innings. Appreciatively, Pulli accepted it and proceeded to down a lusty gulp of hot coffee.

Pitcher's Notes

Many pitchers have been suspected of doctoring the baseball, and some of them have, in fact, been searched for evidence of a foreign substance. Don Sutton was one of them. But he didn't mind. As a matter of fact, he enjoyed the search—but eluded the seizure. When the umpires searched him, they found numerous notes that he had placed in his pockets: "cold," "colder," "freezing," "warm," "hot," "hotter," and "no trespassing."

Dust in the Eye

Sometimes a manager has to make a quick pitching move, and the relief pitcher doesn't have enough time to warm up properly. That was the case when manager Charlie Dressen of the Dodgers hurriedly rushed Clyde King into a game at Ebbets Field. After his preliminary warm-up throws, King simply wasn't ready to pitch.

So shortstop Pee Wee Reese, the team's captain, went into his patented stalling act. He called time out and told the umpires he had a speck of dust in his eye. Then he walked over to third baseman Billy Cox, who proceeded to become a partner in Reese's deceit.

In the meantime, King was supposed to be taking advantage of Reese's ruse by making additional warm-up throws. He became so fascinated with Reese's act, however, that he discontinued his warm-up throws, left the mound, and walked over to third base to see what kind of success Cox was having in removing the speck of dust from Pee Wee's eye.

Maglie the Barber

Today you hear a lot of pitchers complaining because umpires won't let them throw "inside" to the hitter. That wasn't the case in the old days, though.

Some players said that Sal "The Barber" Maglie of the Giants would knock down his own mother on Mother's Day. "I would," he said, "if she was crowding the plate."

Maglie wasn't a loner, but he didn't like to hang out with other players, either. Why not? "I don't want to get to know them," he said. "I might get to like them. Then if the occasion arises, I might not want to throw at them."

More Embarrassment

In 1993, Tom Candiotti was on the mound for the Los Angeles Dodgers when a runner took off for second, attempting a steal. Mike Piazza, who was a rookie catcher that year, came up gunning the ball. The throw was on line, but it never reached second because it struck Candiotti in his derriere.

The knuckleball pitcher later said, "I couldn't help but laugh at that one. I've dodged line drives before, but never a throw from a catcher."

Wrong-Way Corrigan Act

Sid Fernandez inexplicably performed a Wrong-Way Corrigan act back on August 20, 1990. At that time, the lefty pitcher was with the New York Mets. He came to the plate with a man on base and laid down a sacrifice bunt. Then came the chaos. For some reason, Fernandez trotted towards third base.

After a moment he realized his blunder, but it was too late. San Diego not only got a force-out on the runner, they also turned a double play on the disoriented pitcher. It was almost as if he had a momentary case of baseball dyslexia.

E, E, E

Don Slaught calls the next play one of the funniest moments he ever saw on a diamond. It was funny in two ways: It was "odd" funny, and it was also "gallows humor" funny.

Slaught, the catcher that day, relates which happened on July 27, 1988: "I was in New York with the Yankees when Tommy John had...three errors on one play. I think the ball was hit back to him and he bobbled it for an error, then threw it wild to first for another error. The right fielder [Dave Winfield] caught the ball, and threw it in. John cut if off, wheeled and threw it to me, but [he] threw it in the dugout for his third error on one play."

That play made John the first pitcher in the modern era to be guilty of three errors in an inning, and he did it all in a matter of seconds on one zany play.

Torre's Temptation

Joe Torre's Yankees were so hot in 1998, he didn't need to try trick plays. He seems to side with his coach, Chris Chambliss, who said, "There's really no reason to try to reinvent baseball. You want to stay within the basic framework of the game." Torre noted: "Some of those strategies like Don Zimmer's, I just don't have the courage to do."

However, Torre did say there is one play that he's tempted to try. "I'm gonna have the guts to do this one day if we're fortunate to continue to play the way we are. I may, in a lefty–righty situation, have a left-handed pitcher in the game, and he gets a left-hander [batter] out. Then I stick him at first base for an out [bringing in a bullpen righty to pitch to a right-handed hitter, playing the percentages], then bring the lefty back in.

"I think that's fascinating, and I admire the managers who have the courage to do it. I haven't had the courage yet. I'm just afraid something bad's gonna happen."

In the past, managers have made this move. It's believed to have originated with Paul Richards, who placed southpaw starting pitcher Billy Pierce at first base while reliever Harry Dorish retired a righty. After getting the out, Pierce would resume pitching.

Johnny Goryl remembered other managers who would "try to hide a pitcher out there in the outfield, then bring him back in [to pitch as Torre described]." Two other pitchers come to mind who did this: "Sudden" Sam McDowell, a southpaw for the Cleveland Indians, and Kent Tekulve, a right-handed reliever for the Pirates.

Goryl continued, "Back in those days, we only had eight- or nine-man pitching staffs; ten was the most clubs carried. Today we've got thirteen-man staffs, so you don't see this much, now."

Red Hot Chili

In 1995, Sandy Alomar's backup catcher, Tony Peña, and Dennis Martinez recreated one of the most famous trick plays ever. The first time this bit of deception took place was during the 1972 World Series. The Oakland A's were in a situation in which an intentional walk to Johnny Bench made sense. They went through the motions, but at the last second they fired strike three past the befuddled Bench.

Actually, World Series–bound Cleveland did the A's one better —they got away with it on two occasions. Peña and Martinez cooked up the play on their own. Alomar recalled: "Dennis was struggling, and he needed a play to get out of an inning. He had thrown a lot of pitches, and it was a perfect situation to do it. It was a smart play. It worked on Chili Davis, who was very upset about it. They did it one time to John Olerud."

It seems incredible that this play could work twice in a season in this day and age when highlights are constantly played and replayed on television. Alomar concurred, "If I'm a player for a different team, I guarantee you I see that on ESPN, and they wouldn't get me."

Lame Trick

Many baseball fans feel the trick play in which the pitcher fakes a throw towards the runner who is off third base, then swivels, fires, and tries to pick off the runner from first is lame. Somehow, though, it succeeded in 1998.

On the last day in June, the Oakland A's were hosting the San Diego Padres. Entering the top of the ninth, Oakland was clinging to a 12–8 lead. Two outs later, the Padres were rallying. They had scored two runs. Now they had a runner at third with the tying run on first.

With a 2-and-2 count on Mark Sweeney, A's catcher Mike Macfarlane gave reliever Mike Fetters the sign to put on a special pickoff move. Fetters, however, was confused—he had spent the last six years with the Milwaukee Brewers and momentarily mixed up their signals with those of the A's.

So Macfarlane waved his hand in the direction of first, then third to indicate what he wanted. Even after all of that blatant gesturing, Padres runner Ruben Rivera was caught snoozing. Eventually, the rookie Rivera was tagged out trying to make it to second base.

A's manager Art Howe was thinking along the lines of Tony Peña when he called his trick play. "It just didn't seem like anybody was going to make an out, so I said, 'Let's manufacture one,' " commented Howe.

The play was especially mortifying for several reasons. For one, it's foolish to do anything risky (or not pay attention) on the bases in such a situation. After all, this play ended the game and gave the A's a win. Not only that, Rivera was in the game for his running skills—the Padres had just put him in moments earlier as a pinch runner.

Oakland's Jason Giambi observed, "You know the old theory about that play never working? Well, it did today."

When Is a Record Not Really a Record?

When George Edward "Rube" Waddell, the brilliant but eccentric Philadelphia Athletics left-hander, struck out a supposed total of 343 batters in 1904 (Rube went 25–19 in 384 innings of work), that posting stood as a major league record for decades.

Fast-forward to the 1946 season when Bob Feller, fire-balling right-hander of the Cleveland Indians, went on a strikeout binge and wound up with 348 Ks in 371 innings of work as he went 26–15.

Did Feller set a new record? Apparently he did, but whoa! Researchers at the weekly *Sporting News*, led by editor Cliff Kachline, checked through all Philadelphia Athletics box scores of 1904 when Waddell pitched, and discovered that Rube actually fanned 349 batters. The 349 figure was duly recognized, relegating Feller's strikeout total to second place. (Subsequently, of course, Waddell's record was broken, first by Sandy Koufax with 382 Ks in 1965, and then by Nolan Ryan with 383 Ks in 1973.)

Kachline commented on this strange statistical phenomenon: "Official scorers over the years turned in scoresheets with mistakes in them, often simple mistakes like addition. Researchers have gone over these erroneous scoresheets and made the necessary corrections. Thus, the stat has to be changed. Scorers erred because they were usually under deadline pressure. For example, newspapers wanted scores in a hurry so they could be printed in a particular edition."

Kachline also mused, "Sometimes, the official scorers, who were working sportswriters, did not always show up to the game in any kind of condition to do accurate work. No wonder so many mistakes were made."

The Question of Walter Johnson's Victory Total

When fireballing right-hander Walter Johnson retired following the 1927 season after spending 21 years with the Washington Senators, his victory total was given at 413 against 279 losses. Only Cy Young, who won 511 games, has a higher big league victory total than Johnson.

Strangely enough, however, Walter "Big Train" Johnson hadn't finished winning ballgames. Several years after his death in 1946, a number of researchers discovered, by checking all of the box scores of games in which Johnson pitched, that the scorers did not give him credit for three additional victories. Now all the standard references give Johnson 416 total wins.

Johnson's grandson Henry W. Thomas wrote an excellent and well-received biography on the "Big Train" in 1996, appropriately titled *Walter Johnson: Baseball's Big Train*, and said with great family pride, "My granddad was such a great pitcher that he won three major league games after he died."

Thomas added that the "Big Train" also struck out 11 batters after his passing, since his K total was revised from 3497 to 3508.

Walter Johnson was reputed to have thrown a baseball as fast or faster than any other pitcher in baseball history. He was called "Big Train" because it was said that his best pitch traveled faster than any locomotive in existence. Radar guns were not invented during Johnson's era, but most baseball experts who saw "Big Train" in action said they've never seen a pitcher who could match his speed. In today's terms, his fastball traveled a tad over 100 miles per hour. No one else could match that kind of speed.

In his 458-page tome on his grandfather, Henry Thomas repeatedly emphasized again that Walter Johnson made it a practice never to throw close inside to a batter. With his speed, Johnson, one of the true gentlemen of the game, never wanted to hit a batter with his blazing fastball.

Henry Thomas wrote, "If Granddad had pitched tight like so many pitchers of today—including Don Drysdale, who pitches in tight continuously—he could have become a 500-game winner. He never wanted to take a chance of hitting a batter with all that speed. If Walter Johnson threw inside as a matter of strategy, batters would be afraid to dig in. He gave the batters an even chance by not intimidating them, and he still established himself as one of the greatest pitchers of all time."

Two other stats reflect the true greatness of Johnson as a moundsman: his ERA stands at a very skinny 2.17 (good for seventh best on the all-time list), and he threw 110 shutouts (and that is the record). He threw only one no-hitter on July 1, 1920, against the Boston Red Sox.

Extraordinary Mound Feats by Extraordinary Pitchers

Nowadays, most big league pitchers "baby" their arms. In the old days, most major league teams utilized a four-man rotation. Now it's a five-man rotation. That is, hurlers today work every fifth day instead of every fourth day. And these five starters are backed up by a "relief crew" of seven additional pitchers.

The seven relievers are classed into categories: "long men," "set-up men," and "closers." Often times, a reliever will be thrown into the fracas with the purpose of blowing out only a single batter. That "specialist" may be a left-hander whose job it is to get out a left-handed batter in a critical situation late in the game.

Today, moundsmen are taken out of a game if their "pitch count" reaches a certain number of pitches. Some starters are limited to as few as 100 pitches before they're taken out of a game. Very seldom is a starter allowed to hurl as many as 130 pitches per game. A relief pitcher, who often is called upon to "put out fires" two or three times a week, is limited to 30 or perhaps 40 pitches at most. The closer usually comes in to shut down the other side for a single inning. That is true of famed closers like Dennis Eckersley and John Franco. When they go past one inning in a closer situation, they make news.

Strangely, there are now cases where a moundsman appears in about as many games as innings pitched. Take the case of Eckersley, one of the premier relievers of the past 10 or 12 years: In 1993 with the Oakland Athletics, he appeared in 64 games and chalked up only 67 innings pitched; he did have 36 saves—a very good performance. Then with Oakland in 1995, he appeared in 52 games, with only 50 1/3-innings pitched, and a strong 29 games saved. With the St. Louis Cardinals in 1997, he got into 57 games and hurled only 53 innings. He recorded 36 saves, and though his won-lost record was a less-than-mediocre 1–5, that stat doesn't mean all that much. Relievers are paid according to games saved.

John Franco's stats in respect to games played and innings pitched are similar to Eckersley's. While with the New York Mets in 1991, he appeared in 52 games and threw in 55 1/3-innings to go with 30 saves; in 1996 with the Mets, he got into 51 games and threw 54 innings, with 28 saves. Franco is the prototypical closer who rarely goes beyond a one-inning stint. Thus, complete games have become a relative rarity in the big leagues.

Greg Maddux, the star Atlanta Braves right-hander, led the National League in complete games in 1993, 1994, and 1995 with 8, 10, and 10, respectively—low numbers for the leader in that category.

Back in the old days, a reliever was often brought in with the idea that he would finish the game for the starter who was knocked out of the box. In general, lengthy relief appearances have almost gone the way of the carrier pigeon.

Eddie Rommel, the old Philadelphia Athletics star right-hander, spent the last couple of seasons in his 13-year major league career (1920–32) as a reliever, and he chalked up what is generally thought to be the longest relief assignment in big league history.

That came in a July 10, 1932, game against the Cleveland Indians. Athletics starter Lew Krausse was taken out of the game in the first inning when he gave up 3 runs and 4 hits. With two out, Rommel came in to put out the fire. What finally happened was that this turned out to be one of the most unusual and highest-scoring games in major league history. This wild and woolly game lasted for 18 innings before the Athletics won by a fat 18–17 score!

Strangely, Rommel was allowed to go the distance, and he gained the victory with his "tight" relief pitching. In

17 1/3-innings of work, he allowed 14 runs and 29 base hits. Clint Brown, the Indians starting pitcher, was relieved in the late innings by Willis Hudlin and Wesley Ferrell. In this 18-inning marathon, the Indians stroked 33 base hits while the A's hit safely 25 times; an astounding total of 58.

Johnny Burnett, the Indians second baseman, established a record that still stands after nearly 70 years: 9 base hits in a single game in 11 at bats. Indians second baseman Billy Cissell had 4 hits, while first baseman Eddie Morgan hit safely 5 times.

For the A's, first baseman Jimmie Foxx picked up 6 hits in 9 at bats, while left fielder Al Simmons went 5 for 9. No doubt about it, the Indians and the A's had their hitting clothes on during that hot July day in 1932.

The Indians and Athletics were tied 15–15 after 15 innings, but both teams scored a brace of runs in the 16th to knot the score at 17–17. Then the A's scored single runs in the top of the eighteenth to put the game away at 18–17, a football-type score. Nowadays, a game of that length would require about six or so pitchers on each side, but in this monumental clash only five moundsmen saw action.

Rommel had a reputation for being a workhorse, since he had a string of games to his credit where he pitched well beyond nine innings. In an April 13, 1926, game against Washington, for example, he hooked up in a pitching duel with the great Walter Johnson. The Senators squeaked out a 1–0 victory over the Athletics in fifteen innings. Both pitchers went the distance, of course. That wouldn't happen today, because pitchers are rarely allowed to go beyond nine innings. Later on in his career, Rommel became an American League umpire and served for twenty-three seasons (1938–1960) as an A.L. arbiter.

During our years with the Cleveland Indians in the 1950s, we had the chance to speak with Eddie Rommel on several occasions. He was an imposing figure, standing about 6 foot 2 inches and weighing an athletic 200 pounds.

We asked Rommel why pitchers of his era were often able to work so many innings at a single stretch. He answered, "When I broke into pro baseball back in 1918 with the Newark Bears of the International League, we were just coming out of the 'dead ball' era and getting a new, juiced-up, lively ball that made it easier it hit homers. Even after the lively ball came into being in about 1919–20, a lot of hitters liked to continuing to 'slap' the ball and tried more than anything to 'place' relatively short hits. Ty Cobb was basically a slap hitter—I pitched to him many times, and he rarely tried to go for homers.

"Remember, Cobb became a little jealous of Babe Ruth hitting all those homers, and in 1925 Ty said, in effect, 'There's no real trick to hitting homers.' Then he set out to prove his point. In back-to-back games against the St. Louis Browns at Sportsman's Park early in May that year, Ty changed his batting style by taking a full swing. He hit three home runs in the first game, and two more on the following day, giving him five for the two games."

Historians indicated that Cobb was unlucky not to hit seven homers in two days. Two of his shots missed the roof at Sportsmen's Park and dropped for doubles. Rommel went on to say that after that spectacular two-day performance, Cobb went back to his old batting style, which consisted of a snap swing and a quick chop so that he did not have to set himself. That made him able to shift quickly so he could meet any kind of pitch—high, low, inside, outside. The snap swing enabled him to meet the ball squarely even while he was shifting.

Rommel concluded his observations by saying that since pitchers in his era didn't have to worry all that much about game-breaking home runs, they didn't absolutely have to "bear down" on every pitch. He said, "We could pace ourselves." Rommel also emphasized that back in his playing days, pitchers objected to being relieved and strove to remain in the game as long as possible. Thus, starters of that era rolled up more innings per season generally than today's moundsmen. And by the same token, relievers didn't like being relieved, and that's one of the reasons he threw that famed 17 1/3-inning, 29-hit relief performance on the afternoon of July 10, 1932.

Bob Feller Didn't Count His Pitches

From the time Bob "Rapid Robert" Feller broke in with the Indians in mid-season in 1936 as a 17 year old who could heave the baseball 100 miles per hour, he was hailed as the Tribe's best pitcher since old Cy himself. When Feller enlisted in the navy on December 9, 1941 (two days after Pearl Harbor), he had already won 107 games for Cleveland (against 54 losses). No pitcher in baseball history had piled up that many victories that quickly—not even Cy Young himself. Before Feller joined the U.S. Navy, many baseball historians thought that the fireballing right-hander had an even chance of at least approaching Cy Young's monumental victory total. However, Feller's navy duty took him away from baseball for 3 years. He was discharged from the navy toward the end of July 1945. In his first game back, he defeated the Detroit Tigers 4–2 and struck out 12. He obviously regained his old form.

Feller went 5–3 for the last couple of months in the '45 season, and then in 1946 he turned in an almost unbelievable iron-man performance as he rolled up a 26–15 record for the sixth-place Indians. The Indians posted a mediocre 68–86 record that season; thus, Feller won nearly 40% of the team's games.

In 48 games, he pitched an incredible 371 innings, gave up a sparing 277 base hits, and came up with a skinny ERA of 2.18. He made 42 starts and led the league in complete games with an amazing 36. He struck out 348 batters, a figure that was thought to be a record, but later Rube Waddell's strikeout total with the 1904 Philadelphia Athletics was raised to 349.

Feller was thrown into relief situations six times so that he could pitch extra innings in order to have a better chance at breaking Rube Waddell's one-season strikeout record. No starting pitcher in the current era of baseball was ever called upon to go into a game as a reliever.

Still, Feller's regular season stats give only a part of his over-strenuous pitching activities in 1946. Feller wanted to recover the baseball income lost during the nearly 4 years he served in the U.S. Navy. He organized a 30-day nationwide barnstorming tour composed of two teams consisting of major leaguers, plus top players from the Negro professional leagues. During that barnstorming tour, Feller pitched at least 60–70 innings in competition, and thus for the whole of 1946, he threw something like 450 innings. And that's not to say how many innings he threw in spring training in 1946. Nowadays, no pitcher would follow a schedule that outrageously arduous.

Bob Feller would have piled up even more impressive lifetime pitching stats had it not been for a strange accident that occurred in a game he was pitching against the Philadelphia Athletics in June 1947. He fell off the mound—it was a bit slippery since it had been raining that day—and injured his right (pitching) shoulder.

From that point on, Rapid Robert was never quite the same again. He would never be able to throw those 100-plus–mile-per-hour fastballs. But, despite the injury, Bob had a lot of baseball savvy and retained enough good stuff to remain in the majors for another decade. He finished the '47 season at 20–11, and then struggled through the Indians' 1948 pennant with a 19–15 record. While he led the league in strikeouts with 164 in 280 innings, that was well under par for Rapid Robert.

Feller's great ambition was to win a World Series game, but he failed in that quest because of one of the strangest plays in the history of the "Fall Classic." Bob started Game 1 against the Boston Braves at Boston. The game was scoreless through the first seven innings. Then, in the bottom of the eighth, Bill Salkeld singled to open the inning and Braves manager Billy Southworth sent Phil Masi in to run for him. Mike McCormick sacrificed and Eddie Stanky drew an intentional walk. Feller then attempted to pick off

Masi, who had taken a big lead off second. Feller whirled around and fired a bullet to shortstop-manager Lou Boudreau, who cut in behind the runner. Masi slid back and was called safe by base umpire Bill Stewart, although Boudreau protested vehemently that he had made the tag well before the runner had reached the bag. Pitcher Johnny Sain then flied out, but Tommy Holmes came through with a single, to drive in Masi. That was the only run of the game as Boston won the 1–0 squeaker. Films of the play revealed that Boudreau had tagged Masi out before the latter had gotten within 2 or 3 feet of second base.

Feller told us in a 1997 interview, "That was a strange call, all right. Stewart made a mistake because he was not in position to see the tag out. That's the breaks of the game." Feller can be very philosophical about misadventures in baseball. In going the distance, Feller allowed only two hits, walked only three, and struck out two.

After Bill Stewart retired from the National League umpiring crew several years later, he began a new career as a major league scout. And who hired him to that post? Why, none other than the Cleveland Indians. Strange.

In the '48 World Series, Feller got a second chance to win a Series game. In Game 5 at Cleveland Stadium, a clash that drew a standing-room-only crowd of 86,288 (then a record crowd for any big league game), Bob was sent to the showers in the inning with only one man out. He gave up 7 runs on 10 hits, as the Tribe took an 11–5 drubbing. The Indians did take the Series 4 games to 2, with Rapid Robert being the team's only losing pitcher against the Braves.

Feller went 15–14 and 16–11 in the 1949 and 1950 season, respectively—not bad, but not approaching Rapid Robert's past greatness. In 1951, he enjoyed an extraordinary season as he posted a glittering 22–8 record. Many sportswriters were ready to write off Feller as a front-line pitcher at this point in his career, and though Feller's fastball was no longer in the 100-mile-per-hour zone, he made up for it in craftiness. He struck out only 111 batters in 250 innings of work, but he led the American League in wins and in winning percentage with a .733 posting. Even at that fairly late point in his career, Bob threw 16 complete games in 34 starts (more CGs than most league leaders achieve today), including a no-hitter against Detroit on July (the third no-hitter in his career).

Toward mid-season, Feller was involved in just about the strangest of all games in his 18 years as an Indian—a game against the Philadelphia Athletics. The Indians had their hitting clothes on in that clash, and they whomped A's pitchers for 21 runs. The Athletics were no pushovers in the hitting department that day either, as they scored 9 runs. Did Feller get any relief in that slugfest? Absolutely not! He went the distance in picking up the victory. If Feller has been pitching, today he would have been yanked after 5 or 6 innings, just enough to get credit for a win, and the members of the relief corps would have been called in to mop up.

In our 1997 interview with Bob, we asked him why he was permitted to remain on the mound for the entire game when he was getting shelled. He answered, "I asked our manager, Al Lopez, to keep me in the game for a solid purpose. I was experimenting with a couple of new pitches, and I wanted to throw them in game conditions, so it didn't make any difference if I allowed Philadelphia to score a few additional runs, for we had the game wrapped up from the get-go. I know that you can't get away with stuff like that today, but I was glad to work out those pitches in competition and that did help me a lot down the road. And I've got to give credit to Al Lopez, who allowed me to work on those new pitches. And I'm glad to see that Al made it into the Hall of Fame as a manager." Bob concluded, "I must have thrown at least 175 pitches in that game, but then nobody was counting."

Feller dropped to a 9–13 record in 1952, went 10–7 in 1953, and then roared back in 1954 where he posted a 13–3 winning season as a "spot starter." In 19 starts, he threw 9 CGs—not bad. That was the year when the Indians established a major league record for most victories in a season—111 wins against 43 losses.

Feller thought he had another shot at winning his first World Series game against the New York Giants, who finished the season at a comparatively modest 98–59. Unfortunately, the Giants swept the Indians in four straight games with Bob Lemon, Early Wynn, and Mike Garcia taking the losses (Lemon two of them). Manager Lopez had scheduled Feller to pitch the fifth game, but since there was no necessity for a fifth game, Bob never got to pitch in the Series. Feller, philosophical as ever, said, "Stranger and worser things have happened to me before and since. I'm not going to worry about things that I have little or no control over."

Feller wound up his career in the 1955 and 1956 seasons as a spot starter and reliever, and in his 18 years in the majors he came up with a lifetime record of 266 victories and 162 defeats. Through the late 1960s, his strikeout total of 2581 ranked fourth on the all-time list.

While Feller may not have won a World Series game, he did participate in five All-Star games and went 1–0, having been the winning pitcher in the 1946 clash at Fenway Park when the American League clobbered the Nationals 12–0.

Bob Feller certainly wasn't through with baseball after he threw his last pitch for the Cleveland Indians. He continued to appear at old-timers' games and special exhibitions and kept hurling those balls toward the plate into the early 1990s, when he was past 70 years old—or "70 years young," to be more exact in our choice of words. Moreover, he still does his own yard work at his large home in Gates Mills, Ohio, near Cleveland.

David Wells—a Super Babe Ruth Fan

New York Yankees left-handed pitcher David Wells, who helped the Bronx Bombers take the 1998 American League pennant and the World Series crown with an 18–4 regular season record (including throwing a perfect game), has long been noted as a super Babe Ruth fan.

When Wells joined the Yankees in 1997, he asked to wear Babe's retired number 3. When that request was denied, he settled for number 33. From that point, he purchased one of Ruth's game-worn caps at auction for $35,000, and wore it in a 1998 game against the Cleveland Indians. Wells is known in baseball circles as a free spirit.

499 Pitches in One Game!

In a so-called "normal" major league baseball game, an average of 250 pitches are thrown in a nine-inning game, or some 125 by each team. If the game is a high-scoring one, or goes a few extra innings, the count may reach the 300 mark, or in rare cases, 350.

In rarer cases, however, the pitch count may reach stratospheric heights. A case in point came in the September 14, 1998, game played between the Detroit Tigers and Chicago White Sox at Tiger Stadium. This clash turned out to be a 12-inning marathon, as Chicago edged Detroit 17–16 in a wild and woolly affair.

The game was knotted at 12–12 at the end of the regulation 9 innings, and then both clubs scored three runs in the 10th to run the game to 15–15. The White Sox blasted back-to-back homers from Ray Durham and Craig Wilson in the top of the 12th, while the Tigers were able to score only once in their half of the inning, and thus they were nosed out 17–16 in what appears more like a football score.

The Tigers used ten pitchers and the White Sox used eight. Their total of eighteen tied the record for most pitchers in an extra-inning game. The White Sox corps of eight hurlers threw 229 pitches, while the Tigers corps of ten moundsmen threw 270 pitches, or 499 total—a fantastic amount! That comes to at least two games' worth of pitches. The game lasted for 5 hours and 12 minutes, about twice the length of an average game.

Tabulations of pitch counts were not made until recent years, but the Elias Sports Bureau of New York (official statisticians for Major League Baseball) believe that 499 pitches is the record for any game played through 12 innings. Records for pitch counts for games played to 20 innings or so are almost impossible to arrive at.

The number of hits and runs for the Chicago/Detroit donnybrook made the pitch counts run to those high levels. Chicago batters batted out 19 base hits, while the Detroit attack came through with 22 hits. Detroit pitchers walked 11 batters, while Chicago pitchers walked only a single batsman.

The Sox starting pitcher, John Snyder, threw the first 5 innings, gave up 5 runs (4 earned), and worked his pitch count up to 92 before he was relieved. The Tigers starter, Mark Thompson, got through 4 innings, giving up 6 runs (only 2 earned) before he was sent to the showers. Interestingly, he also threw 92 pitches.

The winning pitcher for Chicago was left-hander Scott Eyre, who threw the final two innings, while the losing pitcher for Detroit was Doug Bochtler, who gave up the winning run.

Chicago's Albert Belle and Craig Wilson were the hitting stars of the game, as they drove in five runs apiece. Belle banged out three doubles, to go with his two singles, and went 5 for 8. Wilson, a rookie, went 4 for 7 as he homered twice and singled twice. In that high-scoring game, Belle, a 10-year veteran, passed the 1000-RBI mark.

Jerry Holtzman, veteran Chicago sportswriter, commented, "You never know what's going to happen in a major league baseball game. Depending upon the pitching, the score might wind up at 1–0, or a football-type score at 17–16. There's no use in making pregame predictions."

Lew Burdette Changes Pitching Arm

Lew Burdette, who spent most of his 18-year big league career toiling for the Milwaukee Braves, and who won three games against the New York Yankees in the 1957 World Series to clinch the World Championship for the Braves, was always known as something of a prankster in his playing days. For his 1959 Topps Chewing Gum card, Burdette, a right-handed pitcher, grabbed teammate Warren Spahn's glove and tricked the Topps photographer by posing as a southpaw.

Zany Baseball Cards: Glenn Hubbard and His Pet Python

In a 1998 survey, the weekly *Sports Collectors Digest* named the 1984 Fleer specimen showing Atlanta Braves second baseman Glenn Hubbard with his favorite pet, a 9-foot python, draped around his neck and shoulders, as the zaniest/wackiest baseball card. Hubbard seems to be enjoying the friendship of his reptilian friend, for he has a broad smile on his face. The python, a healthy-looking specimen, obviously has been well fed.

The Saving Win

Can a pitcher get a win and save in the same game? The baseball rule book doesn't cover the possibility.

Answer: A game between the Mets and the Reds, early in the 1986 season, that ultimately went fourteen innings is an example. But let's backtrack first.

With the score tied in the bottom of the tenth inning, Pete Rose hit a single and gave way to pinch-runner Eric Davis, who promptly stole second and third base. Ray Knight, the Mets third baseman, thought that Davis was over-aggressive in his slide into third base, and a fight between the two players, and others, followed. The net result of the fight was that Knight and Davis, in addition to pitcher Mario Soto of the Reds and outfielder Kevin Mitchell of the Mets, were ejected from the game. Darryl Strawberry of the Mets and coach Billy DeMars of the Reds had been ejected in an earlier and separate incident.

Manager Davey Johnson of the Mets didn't have anyone, except a pitcher, to replace Mitchell in the outfield, so he decided to alternate Jessie Orosco, who was pitching, and Roger McDowell, another pitcher, between the mound and the outfield. Each would pitch a full inning and then switch to the outfield for a full inning.

Well, in the top of the fourteenth inning, Ed Hearn of the Mets doubled and Orosco drew a walk from Reds pitcher Carl Willis. Ted Power then came on in relief for Cincinnati and promptly threw a three-run homer to Howard Johnson.

McDowell, who had pitched the thirteenth inning, then stood to be the winning pitcher, and that's the way it turned out when Orosco retired the Reds without a score in the bottom of the fourteenth inning. But suppose, just suppose, Orosco had gotten in trouble in the fourteenth inning, and had to be relieved by McDowell. Then if McDowell had retired the Reds without their tying or winning the game, wouldn't he have technically saved his own win?

Generally a pitcher can get a win or a save, but not both.

Shutout in Relief

Is it possible for a relief pitcher to hurl a shutout?

Answer: Yes, it is. Rule 10.19 f—No pitcher shall be credited with pitching a shutout unless he pitches the complete game, or unless he enters the game with none out before the opposing team has scored in the first inning, puts out the side without a run scoring, and pitches all the rest of the game.

Babe Ruth of the 1917 Red Sox gave way to relief pitcher Ernie Shore under similar circumstances. Ruth walked the Washington Senator lead-off batter, Ray Morgan. When Ruth blasphemously objected to the umpire's fourth-ball call, he was ejected from the game. Shore replaced Ruth, Morgan was thrown out on an attempted steal, and the Red Sox relief pitcher proceeded to retire twenty-six batters in a row.

In essence, Shore recorded not only a shutout, but also the third perfect game in the history of modern-day baseball.

The Crew Cut

A young Houston Astros pitcher with a crew cut constantly loses his cap during his wind-up.

Jim Bouton of the 1964 New York Yankees won two games in that year's World Series against the St. Louis Cardinals. In one of those games, his hat fell to the ground during his wind-up an unofficial thirty-nine times.

Were all of his pitches legal?

Answer: Yes, all his pitches were legal. Rule 2.00.

Knockdown Pitch

Tony Armas of the Red Sox hits home runs the first two times he goes to the plate in a game against the Mariners. The third time up, on a two-oh count, he is hit with a pitch on the elbow by the Seattle southpaw. The home-plate umpire thinks that the Mariners pitcher hit Armas deliberately, and he also feels that the Seattle manager ordered the beanball.

What punitive power does the umpire possess?

Answer: The umpire, when he thinks that the pitcher has hit a batter, may remove both the hurler and the skipper from the game. Rule 8.02 [d-1].

Jerry Koosman and manager Joe Torre of the Mets got ejected from a game for the above reason in 1978. Before 1978, when the new rule came into effect, it was more common for the pitcher to be fined and/or suspended.

One Off the Mound

Late in the 1986 season, the Yankees held a 5-4 lead over the visiting Indians in the bottom of the eighth inning. The Bombers had Rickey Henderson on second base and Don Mattingly on first base. Mike Easler was at the plate with two out.

Pitcher Frank Wills, on a two-two pitch, tried to throw the ball too fine and bounced the pitch in front of catcher Chris Bando. The Indian backstop blocked the ball, but it caromed off him toward the Yankee dugout. Henderson and Mattingly quickly moved up a base. But the Yankee television announcer got audibly excited, thinking that the Bombers should possibly get more runs if the ball went into the dugout.

Would they?

Answer: No. Runners can advance only one base on a pitch that goes out of play. Rule 7.05 h—APPROVED RULING. The same rule would apply if the ball had gone through a hole in the backstop or if it had become lodged in the mesh of the screen.

Errors and Earned Runs

Frank Tanana of the Angels gets off to an unlucky start. In the first inning, he has runners on first and second base with two out when Alan Trammell of the Tigers hits a catchable pop fly, in foul territory, to the California third baseman. But the fielder misjudges the ball, and it falls to the ground in foul territory, untouched. Trammell, given a reprieve, proceeds to double both runners across home plate.

Do the runs count against the pitcher's earned run average?

Answer: Yes, they do. The third baseman, because he misjudged the ball and did not touch it, was not given an error on the play.

Lefty Steve Carlton of the Phillies struggled through the 1986 season. Third baseman Mike Schmidt didn't make Carlton's season any easier when he misjudged a pop fly under similar circumstances midway through the year. Because he misjudged the ball, he didn't get charged with an error. The next batter doubled two runs home. Carlton got charged with two tough earned runs.

The Good-Hitting Pitcher

Tommy Byrne, a good-hitting pitcher in the 1950s, used to pinch-hit periodically. One day he pinch-hit for Phil Rizzuto, his Yankee teammate who was batting eighth in the lineup. Then, in the next half inning of the game he entered the contest as a relief pitcher. Billy Hunter substituted for Rizzuto in the lineup.

By the way, where would Byrne and Hunter bat in the lineup?

Answer: Byrne would bat in the eighth spot and Hunter would hit in the pitcher's position. Rule 3.03 and 4.04.

Balk or Pickoff?

Dave Righetti of the Yankees is the pitcher in relief, and Rickey Henderson of the A's is the runner on first base. Righetti throws five consecutive pick-off attempts to first baseman Don Mattingly. In the meantime, Henderson extends his lead and finally Righetti, standing on the rubber in the set position, snaps a pick-off throw to Mattingly without stepping toward first base. Mattingly tags Henderson out.

Balk or pickoff?

Answer: Balk. Rule 8.01 c—The pitcher must step toward first base ahead of the throw. Henderson is awarded second base.

In reality, Righetti has a good snap pick-off move to first base. But he first steps back off the rubber with his pivot foot, thereby becoming an infielder, and he makes the throw with impunity.

Experimental Play

In an attempt to speed up games, the American League in 1911 experimented with a rule that prohibited pitchers from making warm-up pitches between innings.

During a game between the Red Sox and the Athletics, Boston moundsman Ed Karger snuck in a few warm-up tosses while his teammates were trotting out to their positions.

Stuffy McInnis, the Athletics' first baseman who was on deck at the time, took advantage of the situation. He sneaked into the batter's box and smashed one of Karger's pitches off the fence in left field. McInnis then rounded the bases with an inside-the-park home run.

Did it count?

Answer: Under the rules of the time, the umpires concluded, the play was a legal one. It was Karger who got penalized for an "illegal" attempt.

The Balk before the Balk

The Cleveland Indians have a runner on second base when the Detroit Tiger pitcher commits a balk. During the pitch, however, batter Cory Snyder hits a ground ball to the third baseman, who first bluffs the runner back to second base and then throws the ball late to first baseman Dave Bergman.

Is the balk nullified because the batter-runner was safe?

Answer: No. Each runner, including the batter-runner, must advance in order to nullify a balk call. The umpire moves the runner to third and directs the batter to hit again. Rule 8.05, PENALTY.

One or More?

Rickey Henderson, the runner at first base for the Oakland A's, gets a quick break toward second base during an attempted steal.

The pitcher, whose stride foot has already made his move toward the plate and has broken the plane of the rubber throws off-balance and wildly to first base. As the ball rolls down the right-field line, in foul territory, the home-plate umpire signals a balk while Henderson circles the bases and scores.

Does the arbiter return Henderson to second base on the balk award, or does he allow the run?

Answer: He permits Henderson to score. Rule 8.05 APPROVED RULING—In cases where pitchers balk and throw wildly, either to a base or home plate, a runner or runners may advance beyond the base to which they were entitled at their own risk.

Traded

Eddie Lopat is pitching for the Yankees against the Orioles when the game is suspended because of darkness. Before the game can be resumed, Lopat is traded to Baltimore. Coincidentally, it is his turn to pitch when the suspended game is resumed, weeks later. Can Lopat pitch for a team that he pitched against in that very same game, and can he pitch against a team he hurled for in that very same contest?

Answer: The answer to both questions is yes. Rule 4.12 d—A player who was not with the club when the game was suspended may be used as a substitute, even if he has taken the place of a player no longer with the club who would not have been eligible because he had been removed from the lineup before the game was suspended.

Ball in Glove

The Tiger batter hits a hard smash back at veteran Yankee pitcher Tommy John. John catches the ball but he can't extricate it from the webbing of his glove. In frustration he runs toward first base and finally tosses the glove with the ball in it to first baseman Don Mattingly, who steps on the bag before the batter-runner reaches it.

Is the Tiger batter-runner out?

Answer: Since the tossing of the glove with the ball in it violated no rule, the Tiger batter-runner is out. Rule 6.05j.

The Quick Hook

Casey Stengel, managing in the National League, often pinch-hit in the first inning. If he got the chance to go for the big inning early, he would.

Let us say that three runs have scored, the bases are loaded with two out, and he pinch-hits for the pitcher in the top of the first inning.

Good move?

Answer: No. The umpire can't permit the substitution. He has to make the pitcher hit. Rule 3.05a—The pitcher named in the batting order handed the umpire-in-chief as provided in rule 4.01 shall pitch to the first batter until such batter is put out or reaches first base, unless the pitcher sustains an injury. In the American League, since the DH (Designated Hitter) rule passed, the pitcher never bats.

The Slip Pitch

Every once in a while, a hurler will experience a slip pitch. For example, the pitcher, with no one on base, runs a three-two count on the batter before a pitch slips out of his hand and dribbles twenty feet toward the plate. Has the pitcher walked the batter? If the pitcher does the same thing with a runner on third base, is it a balk? Does the runner at third base score?

Answer: In the first example it is no pitch, no walk. A pitch with no one on base has to cross a foul line to be considered a pitch. Rule 8.01 d—With men on base, the same "pitch" is a balk. The runner at third base scores.

Raising the Mound

Attempting to confuse the opposing pitching staff, the home team adds four inches in height to its pitching mound. Can the host team alter the height of the mound? Or is the height of the mound regulated by major-league rule?

Answer: Before 1950, mounds could be as high as fifteen inches in height above the basic baseball diamond. They could also be lower, though. In 1950 the height was standardized at fifteen inches. In 1969 it was reduced to ten inches flat. Rule 1.04.

The Big Wind-Up

Nolan Ryan of the Texas Rangers, with a large lead in the ninth inning, takes a big, slow wind-up with Tony Fernandez of the Toronto Blue Jays on first base. By the time Ryan releases the pitch, Fernandez rounds second base.

In the meantime, batter George Bell hits a ground ball to the Ranger shortstop, whose errant throw winds up in the stands behind first base.

Does Fernandez score or stop at third base?

Answer: When Fernandez broke for second base, Ryan was on the rubber in pitching position, so Tony is considered to have been on first base when the play began. Consequently, he is only entitled to third base, and Bell is motioned to second base. Rule 7.05 g.

The Quick Pitch

Rickey Henderson takes a lot of time setting up in the batter's box before he is ready to hit. The California Angel's, this one day, is a quick worker, and he doesn't like to lose his rhythm, so he throws a quick pitch to the surprised Henderson. The hurler hopes to accomplish two things with his quick pitch: first, he wants to get ahead in the count and second, he wants to send a message to Henderson to be ready to hit the next time he steps into the batter's box.

Does he succeed?

Answer: No. Rule 2.00, ILLEGAL PITCH, A QUICK RETURN PITCH, 8.01 d—The batter should be granted reasonable time to assume his stance. The umpire should hold up his hand, signaling the pitcher not to deliver, until the batter is set. If the moundsman makes an illegal pitch with the bases unoccupied, it shall be called a ball. An illegal pitch when runners are on base is a balk.

The No Throw

Dennis Rasmussen of the San Diego Padres has a unique move to second base. Working from the stretch position, he lifts his lead leg straight up in the air, suspends it there briefly, and then spins clockwise and throws to second base. Once, when he was pitching with the Yankees, he picked off Gary Pettis of the Angels with such a move. Then, in his next outing, he made the same move towards a runner at second base, stepped towards the bag with his lead foot, but didn't throw the ball. He simply bluffed the runner back to the base.

Was that a balk?

Answer: No. Rule 8.05 c—The pitcher is to step directly toward a base before throwing to that base, but he is not required to throw (except to first base only) because he steps.

Obstruction or Interference?

Lenny Dykstra of the Phillies, with runners on first and second base with no out, pops up a bunt between the pitcher's mound and the first-base line. The Padre pitcher dives in fair territory for the ball, deflects it into foul ground, and in the process rolls into Dykstra, who falls to the ground.

In the meantime, catcher Benito Santiago picks up the ball and throws it to the first baseman for the out.

Legal play?

Answer: No. The umpire calls obstruction on the pitcher. As soon as the Padre moundsman bumps into Dykstra, without the ball in his hand, the ball is dead. Dykstra is awarded first base, and the other runners are awarded the bases to which the umpire thinks they would have advanced if there had not been any obstruction. (Rule 2.00—OBSTRUCTION and 7.06a). The Phillies have the bases loaded with no one out.

Wrong Language

Salome Barojas of the White Sox was pitching one day with the bases loaded. Jim Fregosi, who was managing the Sox at that time, sent one of his coaches to the mound to speak to Barojas. When the coach got to the mound, however, he realized that he couldn't speak Spanish, so he signaled to the Spanish-speaking third baseman to come over to the mound to act as an interpreter.

Was this legal?

Answer: That constituted a second visit to the mound during the same at bat. Barojas had to leave the game.

Back to the Mound

A pitcher must throw to at least one complete batter, or retire the side, before he may be removed from a game, right?

Home-plate umpire Greg Kosc had trouble with that rule during a 1989 game between the Twins and the Red Sox. The host Twins were defeating the Red Sox that night, and they had two runners on base with one out. At that point Minnesota manager Tom Kelly inserted left-handed-hitting Jim Dwyer to pinch hit. Red Sox manager Joe Morgan countered by bringing in left-hand pitcher Joe Price. Dwyer wanted to bunt the first pitch, but at the last moment he tried to check his swing. But Kosc called the pitch a strike, Dwyer argued the call vehemently, and the umpire ended up throwing him out of the game.

Kelly then sent right-handed-hitting Carmen Castillo up to the plate to take Dwyer's place, so Morgan naturally brought in a right-handed-pitcher, Mike Smithson, to face Castillo. After Smithson had finished, Kelly informed the umpires that a pitcher has to face one complete spot in the batting order, regardless of how many players occupy that spot.

Crew chief umpire Barnett sent Smithson back to the

bullpen and directed Price, who was in the dugout, to return to the mound and conclude pitching to that spot in the lineup. Price proceeded to strike out Castillo.

Tough Call

Let's begin with a very difficult call, one that confronted San Diego Padres manager Preston Gomez back on July 21, 1970. His pitcher, Clay Kirby, was methodically mowing down the New York Mets. Through 8 innings, the Mets had not chalked up a hit.

Now comes the dilemma. Despite the no-hitter, Kirby was losing, 1–0. In the bottom of the eighth, the host Padres came to bat, and, with two men out, Kirby was due to hit. What did Gomez do?

Did he pinch hit for Kirby in an effort to rev up some offense, or did he let Kirby remain in the game so the 22-year-old sophomore pitcher could try to secure his no-hitter?

Answer

Gomez made a gutsy move that was criticized a great deal—he lifted Kirby for a pinch hitter. What really gave second-guessers ammunition for their anger was the fact that the move made no difference. The Padres went on to drop the game 3–0, and the bullpen went on to lose the no-hit bid. Through 1998, the Padres were one of just three teams (not counting 1998 expansion clubs) that had never recorded a no-hitter. (The others are the Mets and Rockies.)

Change of Scenario

If you voted emotionally to let Kirby try for the no-hitter and felt the choice was easy, you aren't alone—tons of fans feel this way. Now, however, let's change the scenario a bit. Would you remain as liberal if the game had entered the bottom of the ninth and was scoreless? Are you still sticking with him? Let's further assume Kirby is tiring a bit, and his pitch count is rapidly climbing.

Finally, for stubborn fans clinging to the thought of staying with Kirby, would it change your mind if you had a hot pinch hitter salivating, anxious to come off the bench? This time, there's no right or wrong answer—it's your call.

Similar Scenario

In 1974, the Houston Astros manager faced a situation much like the Clay Kirby near no-hitter. Don Wilson had worked his way through 8 innings of no-hit ball and was due up to bat in the 8th inning. The manager lifted Wilson for a pinch hitter. Moments later, the new pitcher, Mike Cosgrove, began the ninth by issuing a leadoff single to Cincinnati's Tony Perez for the only hit they'd get that day. The Reds also wound up winning the game, 2–1. The punch line here is that the Astros manager was none other than Preston Gomez.

Perhaps there's no connection, but Gomez managed Houston again in 1975 for part of the season (127 games), then went nearly five years before being hired again as a big league manager. After 90 games as the Cubs' manager, he never had a job as a major league skipper again.

Was Vida Feeling Blue?

Oakland A's manager Alvin Dark had a dilemma similar to Gomez's. On the final day of the 1975 season, Dark sent his ace, Vida Blue (with his 21 wins), to the mound. The A's had already clinched the Western Division, so Dark decided to have Blue pitch just 5 innings, then rest him for the upcoming playoffs.

At the end of those 5 innings, Blue had a no-hitter going. Dark didn't change his mind, though. He went to the bullpen for Glenn Abbott, who worked a hitless 6th inning. In the seventh, Dark brought in Paul Lindblad before turning the chores over to his closer, Rollie Fingers, to wrap it up. The quartet of pitchers managed to throw a highly unusual no-hitter with Blue getting the win. This game marked the first no-hitter by four men.

Intentional Walk Lunacy

Intentional walks are a big part of a manager's strategic repertoire. Frequently, with first base unoccupied, a team will deliberately walk a dangerous hitter and take its chances that the next batter will hit the ball on the ground. If he does and the defense turns a double play, a volatile situation is defused, and the team is out of a dangerous inning.

Would a situation ever call for intentionally walking a man with the bases loaded?

Answer: As is the case with many of the plays that follow, this call is based on opinion. However, 99.99 percent of all the managers who ever filled out a lineup card would feel such a move was positive proof of temporary insanity. Believe it or not, such a move has taken place in a big league game, and on more than one occasion!

Two Intentional Incidents

The most recent occasion was on May 28, 1998, when the San Francisco Giants faced the Arizona Diamondbacks. The score was 8–6 in the bottom of the ninth. With two outs and the bases loaded, Arizona manager Buck Showalter ordered an intentional walk to the always dangerous Barry Bonds.

After Bonds had moseyed down to first, the Giants were within one run. However, the next batter, Brent Mayne, made Showalter look good by lining out to right fielder Brent Brede on a payoff pitch, ending the contest.

The Second Bold Intentional Walk

Showalter wasn't the only manager who made a brazen strategic move in 1998. On May 24 in the 14th inning of a chaotic game, San Francisco manager Dusty Baker definitely went against accepted baseball wisdom. In the top of the 14th, with the game still tied, Giants pitcher Jim Poole handled St. Louis hitters Ron Gant and Delino

De-Shields with no problem. Mark McGwire stepped up to the plate, and that's when it happened. Baker ordered an intentional walk to the hot-hitting Mark McGwire.

Baker was deliberately allowing the potential game-winning run to reach base. Traditionalists were apoplectic, but Baker had his reasons for the walk. First of all, anybody who followed the game in 1998 knew McGwire was one bad dude. In fact, he had already homered in the 12th inning. That gave him a major league-leading 24 blasts. With a full week to go in May, he was tied for the record for the most homers ever hit by the end of of that month. (Later, he did break that record.)

In addition, Baker was following the baseball adage that you just don't let certain superstars beat you—you take the bat out of their hands. On that day, Baker took McGwire's bat away three times with intentional walks.

When Ray Lankford followed with a single, things appeared to be shaky. However, Poole managed to strike out Willie McGee to end the inning without further damage. Ultimately, the move worked since the Giants went on to win 9–6 in 17 innings. Poole said of the walk, "Your first instinct is like, 'No!' Then you realize it's him [McGwire], and you say, 'Oh, well, I guess so.' He's doing pretty good right now." Clearly that was an understatement.

Veteran pitcher Orel Hershiser captured the spirit of the event. He said, "Walk McGwire with nobody on? That's a legend. Jim Poole and Dusty Baker will be trivia, and McGwire will be the legend."

Walks from the Past

The last time prior to the Bonds bases-loaded intentional walk incident that such a tactic was used in the majors was on July 23, 1944, when the Giants' player-manager, Mel Ott, faced the Cubs and Bill Nicholson. The Cubs strongman had homered three times in the first game of the twinbill, and wound up with six homers in the series by the time Ott made his unusual move. Nicholson's hot streak pushed him by Ott for the league leadership for homers. All this set the stage, and in the second game of a doublcheader at the Polo Grounds, Ott, with a 10–7 lead in the eighth inning, gave Nicholson (who represented the go-ahead run) a free pass with the bases loaded and two outs. Ott's logic was, it's better to give up one run than four on a grand slam. For the record, the move worked, as the Giants held on to win, 12–10.

Legend has it that Hub Pruett walked Babe Ruth on purpose with the bases jammed on June 14, 1923, but reliable sources say this isn't true.

Nap Lajoie was actually the very first man to draw a bases-loaded intentional walk. On May 23, 1901, the White Sox led the Athletics 11–7 in the ninth, but with the bases loaded and nobody out, player-manager Clark Griffith left the bench and became the relief pitcher. At that point he decided to give the walk to Lajoie, who represented the tying run. Lajoie would hit over .400 that year, but had the bat taken out of his hands on that occasion. The decision to walk him paid off when Griffith got the next three batters. So, while the move is extremely rare, it has been done. Still, don't hold your breath waiting for the next time a manager pulls this tactic out of his cobwebbed bag of tricks.

Yet Another Unique Intentional Walk

Under any circumstances, would you walk the leadoff hitter if it meant putting the winning run on base or at the plate?

Answer: You probably shouldn't, but it has been done. Frank Howard, a star for the Los Angeles Dodgers and Washington Senators, couldn't recall specific names, but he stated, "I've seen a manager, against an especially hot hitter that could beat him in a tough ball game, intentionally walk him to lead off an inning, putting the winning run on base." Now that's a brazen move, folks.

Back to Ott

Ott, by the way, was no stranger to drawing walks. He drew five walks in a game four times during his career—a record that still stands. He also shares a record for coaxing seven straight walks over a three-day period in 1943. Additionally, from 1936 through 1942, he compiled 100-plus bases on balls, also an all-time big league record.

Then there was the time he drew six walks in a double-header. He was playing against the Phillies on October 5, 1929, and, as the season was winding down, he was shooting for the home run title. Chuck Klein of the Phillies was also trying to win that crown. So, Klein's manager, Burt Shooton, instructed his pitchers to pitch around Ott. Klein, in part thanks to the Shooton strategy, went on to lead the league in homers.

When Not Pitching Is Good

Along the same lines as the Ott intentional walk issue, sometimes not pitching to a slugger or a particularly hot hitter is as much a case of good strategy as, say, knowing when to yank a tiring pitcher from the hill.

In 1969, when San Francisco first baseman Willie McCovey was wielding a lethal bat, opposing managers avoided him as if he were a coiled, angry python. Not only did "Stretch" go on to win the National League's Most Valuable Player award (45 HR, 126 RBI, and a lofty .656 slugging percentage), he was awarded first base intentionally a record 45 times as well. That works out to about three intentional walks every 10 games.

Foxx Hunt

Consider, too, what American League managers did to Jimmie Foxx. During his 20-year career, spent almost entirely in the "Junior Circuit," Foxx amassed 534 homers, enough even now to rank in the all-time top ten. Knowing how powerful "Double X" was, managers often had their pitchers work around him.

On June 16, 1938, Foxx, by then with the Boston Red Sox, was well on his way to an incredibly productive season that included a .349 average, 50 home runs, and 175 runs batted in. On that day, the feared Foxx was issued six walks during a 9-inning game, still good for a major league record. While the walks were not officially listed as intentional walks, it's pretty obvious that pitchers worked him quite carefully. Again, not pitching can be a wise move.

To Pitch or Not to Pitch, That Is the Question

After all the talk about pitching or not pitching to blistering hot hitters, here's a real-life case. In the best-of-seven National League Championship Series (NLCS) back in 1985, the Los Angeles Dodgers squared off against the St. Louis Cardinals. The winner would head to the World Series.

The NLCS stood at 3 games to 2 in favor of the Cardinals. The Dodgers had to have a win. They were leading 5–4 as the top of the 9th inning rolled around. Then a critical situation developed. With two men out and runners on second and third, the Redbirds mounted a major threat. Even a single would probably score two, giving St. Louis the lead.

To make matters worse for the jittery Dodgers, the batter was Jack Clark, the Cardinals cleanup hitter, who had already crushed 22 homers and driven in 87 runs that year in just 126 games to go with his .281 batting average.

Other Factors

Clark, the right-handed first baseman, was 6 feet, 2 inches tall and weighed 205 pounds. Dodger manager Tommy Lasorda knew he could walk Clark since first base was open. That would set up a force play at every base and allow the bullpen to face the number-five hitter instead of Clark.

Lasorda had already decided he was sticking with his reliever Tom Niedenfuer. The big (6 feet, 5 inches; 225 pounds) righty had entered the game when starter Orel Hershiser got in a tough spot after recording just one out in a 3-run 7th inning for the Cards. Niedenfuer was 7–9 out of the bullpen. He had 19 saves and an earned run average of 2.71 on the season.

Lasorda's dilemma was whether to issue a walk to Clark or to have Niedenfuer go right at Clark to secure the final out.

Keep in mind three final bits of information: First, Niedenfuer had absorbed the loss in the fifth game of the NLCS just two days earlier. In that game, he had surrendered a 9th-inning game-winning home run to Ozzie Smith, of all people. Smith was just starting to shed his "good glove, no stick" label in 1985, but even then he had hit just six regular-season homers.

Second, the Dodger reliever had already whiffed Clark to help calm down a St. Louis uprising in the 7th inning. If he had Clark's number, it might be best to defy common strategic practice and pitch to Clark.

Third, if the Dodgers gave Clark a walk, the next batter they'd have to face would be a lefty, the 24-year-old outfielder Andy Van Slyke, coming off a .259, 13 home run, 55 RBI season. In such a situation, what would your call be?

The Actual Call and Results

Lasorda felt they could get Clark out. If your call was to walk Clark, you can gloat since Clark teed off on the very first pitch, jacking it out of the park for a pennant-winning home run. The Dodgers did have three outs left, but they were dead, going out one-two-three in the bottom of the ninth.

Incidentally, according to one version of this story, Lasorda instructed his reliever to pitch carefully to Clark, giving him an "uninten-tional-intentional walk." Still, a straightforward order for an intentional pass seems to have been the proper call.

While Lasorda's call took a lot of nerve, it also certainly went against the book. When you make such a call and things work out, you look like a genius. However, you wear the goat's horns when the call backfires.

Speaking of Intimidation

Some of the greatest artists in that field were also among the game's greatest pitchers. If you were a major league manager, wouldn't you like to have some of the following characters on your staff?

• Dizzy Dean. Although he was considered a colorful guy, he could also get serious. Take the time he noticed a hitter digging in while settling into the batter's box. Dean glared at him, then bellowed in true Clint Eastwood "make-my-day" fashion, "You comfortable? Well, send for a groundskeeper and a shovel 'cause that's where they're going to bury you."

• Nolan Ryan. If he hit you with a pitch, you knew it would hurt. Jay Buhner, a bona fide slugger with the Seattle Mariners, once said of Ryan, "Nolan used to come up and stare you down."

• Early Wynn. He's supposed to have said that he'd knock down his own grandmother if she were crowding the plate, but that was probably apocryphal. However, Wynn was one fiery competitor.

• Don Drysdale. His philosophy of intimidation was quite simple: If the opposing team knocked down one of Drysdale's Dodger teammates, he'd knock down two of the opposing team's batters.

Clearly, the question about wanting such men on your staff is rhetorical. Nevertheless, intimidation is a very real, almost tangible part of baseball's hidden strategy.

Pickoff Chicanery

Say Ken Griffey, Jr. of the Seattle Mariners pounded a ball into the right field corner. The ball kicked around a bit, and Griffey kept digging around the base paths, sliding into third in a cloud of dust. Let's further imagine he called time-out to brush the dirt from his uniform.

Now the third baseman tosses the ball back to the pitcher, a righty. The pitcher straddles the rubber for a moment, then, seeing Griffey stroll off the bag, throws over. Griffey is doomed—or is he? You're the umpire. What's the call?

Answer: It is not an out; Griffey can stay at third base. In order for play to resume after a time-out, the pitcher must come in contact with the rubber, not merely straddle it. Thus, time is still out, and the play never happened.

A Tricky Oldie

The year is 1930, and the pitcher is Burleigh Grimes, a man who later retired with 270 career wins. Grimes goes to his mouth and loads up the baseball with a nasty concoction of chewing tobacco and saliva. If you were working that game, what would your call be?

Answer: Absolutely nothing. Although the spitball was out-lawed in 1920, there was a grandfather clause that permitted a handful of pitchers to continue to throw their specialty pitch. The last man to legally throw a spitter was none other than Hall-of-Famer Burleigh "Ol' Stubblebeard" Grimes in 1934.

Bounces

Back in 1993, Damon Buford was in the Orioles batter's box facing pitcher Matt Young. A pitch to Buford hit the ground and bounced up towards the plate. Buford didn't care that it one-hopped its way to the strike zone; he swung and hit a comebacker to Young. When Young lobbed the ball to first, Buford was ruled out. Did the umpire blow this call? Should it have been a dead ball and no pitch?

Answer: The call was correct. Herb Score, a 20-game winner in 1956, said he once "threw one up to the plate that bounced, and the batter swung and hit a home run." Even if a batter is hit by a pitch that hits the dirt first, it counts. Such a runner would be given first base.

The Waiting Game

With no runners on base, Angels fireballing reliever Troy Percival came into a game to face the Baltimore Orioles. Percival, like a less dramatic version of Al "The Mad Hungarian" Hrabosky, went behind the mound to gather his thoughts. The home plate umpire timed Percival, said he violated a delay of game rule, and called an automatic ball on him. Can this happen?

Answer: Yes. The rule states that with no men on base, a pitcher has just 20 seconds to deliver a pitch. Thus, the relief pitcher was behind in the count, 1-and-0, before even throwing a pitch.

The umpires probably invoked this little-known rule because Percival is notorious for such tactics. The Orioles manager, Ray Miller, said of the relief pitcher, "This guy warms up, nervous as hell, walks around the mound, says prayers, bows behind the mound, looks over the center field fence, and everything else. They got tired of it and called ball one."

No-Hit Glory

Has a pitcher ever come up with a no-hitter during his very first start?

Answer: Amazingly, yes. More amazingly, the pitcher wasn't very good at all. Alva "Bobo" Holloman had pitched exclusively out of the bullpen. Then, after begging owner Bill Veeck to give him a start, he came up with his gem back in 1953. Although Holloman succeeded that day, his luck didn't last; he was gone from the majors for good just a short time later that same year.

His career statistics are paltry: 3 wins versus 7 losses, an ERA of 5.23, and twice as many walks (50) as batters struck out. His no-hitter was his only complete game ever.

The 300 Club

Certain numbers have a magical quality in baseball. For example, as a rule, if a hitter connects for 500 homers, he's headed for the Hall of Fame. For pitchers, making it into the 300-Win Club—a highly exclusive circle of stars—is a coveted goal. Has a pitcher ever managed to lose 300 games?

Answer: Yes, and ironically the man to lose the most games in big league history (313 to be precise) is the same man whose name graces the trophy that personifies pitching excellence—Cy Young. So the award given for pitching excellence actually has its origin with the game's biggest loser. Of course, to be fair, Young also won a staggering 511 games, the most ever in the annals of the game. The next highest win total is nearly 100 less than that—Walter Johnson's 416 victories.

By the way, the only other man to drop 300 decisions was an obscure pitcher from the late nineteenth century named Pud Galvin. This right-hander made it to the Hall of Fame, as did Young. Galvin pitched only 14 years, yet he won 361 games and had such unusual numbers as a 46–29 won–lost record in 1883 and 46–22 the next season. Imagine, he won 92 games in just two years—that's four and a half to five years' worth of toil for a good pitcher today. Of course, his 51 losses over that two-year span would also take quite a few years for a good pitcher to reach today.

27-Game Winner with a Loser?

Has a team that finished in last place ever produced a 27-game winning pitcher? Could a lousy team score enough runs and support a pitcher well enough for him to have a chance to win 27 games?

Answer: This has happened once. Steve Carlton, one of the greatest lefties ever, pitched for the hapless Philadelphia Phillies of 1972 and accomplished just that. The Phils finished sixth in the six-team National League East Division that year with a 59–97 record (.378 win–loss percentage). They were so far behind first-place Pittsburgh that they needed a spyglass and a crow's nest to see the Pirates.

Despite that, Carlton went 27–10, good for an astronomical .730 won–loss percentage. He accounted for nearly half the Phillies wins that year (45.8 percent to be exact). His ERA was a minuscule 1.97 over a workhorse 346 1/3 innings. That's not all. He also fanned 310 men while walking only 87. He even chalked up 30 complete games in registering one of the most dominant years ever. His reward was a unanimous Cy Young Award, making him the only pitcher from a last-place team to ever earn that trophy.

Switch Pitcher?

Has a modern-day pitcher ever thrown with both arms during a major league game?

Answer: Yes, and it happened in the not-too-distant past. As the 1995 season came to an end, Greg Harris, a Montreal Expo right-handed pitcher (also listed as a switch hitter), faced the Cincinnati Reds. He threw a scoreless 9th inning while pitching with both arms. Naturally, he threw left-handed to lefty batters and right-handed to righties.

Prior to Harris, one player, with the poetic name of Ed Head, also used both arms in an inning. He did so because he had injured the arm he normally used.

World Series Excellence

Was there ever a World Series in which every game was decided by a shutout?

Answer: Indeed there was. During the dead-ball era, specifically in 1905, the New York Giants won the Series in five contests. They did it mainly by riding their ace pitcher, Christy Mathewson. He won games one, three, and the finale by scores of 3–0, 9–0, and 2–0, as he fired 27 straight shutout innings.

The other Giants win belonged to Joe McGinnity, known as Iron Man, who produced a 1–0 beauty in the fourth game. McGinnity even pitched well in the only loss to the Philadelphia Athletics, a shutout fired by Chief Bender. As a matter of fact, only three men pitched for New York in that Series, and the third man did so for just 1 inning. Their combined ERA for the Series was invisible at 0.00! Philadelphia scored just three runs in all.

Better Than Perfect

This question involves a very famous game that took place in the 1950s. Did a pitcher ever throw a perfect game that went beyond 9 innings?

Answer: Even though the above question seems to give away the answer, this question, like a Gaylord Perry pitch, is loaded. While it's true Harvey Haddix threw a perfect game that went into the 13th inning back in 1959, a bizarre ruling by baseball officials in 1991 took away his perfect game status. The rule states that in order for a pitcher to get credit for a no-hitter, he must pitch at least 9 innings and pitch a complete game without surrendering a hit. Therefore, what most experts agree was the most perfect game ever is not recognized as such.

Here's what happened on that historic night. Haddix, a diminutive lefty for the Pirates, was perfect through 12 innings against the Milwaukee Braves. Felix Mantilla led off the 13th and reached base on a throwing error by Pirates third baseman Don Hoak. Eddie Mathews then sacrificed the runner to scoring position. That prompted Pittsburgh manager Danny Murtaugh to issue an intentional walk to the dangerous Hank Aaron, setting up a double play.

Pandemonium ensued when Joe Adcock homered. But, due to yet another baseball rule, he only received credit for a double. The reason he was robbed of a home run isn't quite as bizarre as the ruling that hurt Haddix, however. Aaron saw the ball soaring deep and figured it would drop near the fence, so he touched second base, but he never bothered to go to third. As Adcock rounded the bags and touched third base, he was technically guilty of passing a runner and, therefore, received credit for two bases, not four. Adcock also received just one run batted in, instead of three.

Martinez Also Robbed

In 1995, Montreal Expos pitcher Pedro Martinez also got ripped off by the new no-hitter rule. Facing the Padres, he was perfect through 9 innings. Shortly thereafter, when Bip Roberts doubled to lead off the tenth, the perfect game was gone. Martinez then gave way to closer Mel Rojas, who retired the last three batters. The Expos went on to win a 1–0 classic.

Quotations

Although he probably wasn't trying to be humorous, this good ol' country boy once said, "They X-rayed my head and didn't find anything."

—*Dizzy Dean*

Soon after being traded, a disgruntled player, asked about the condition of his shoulder, replied, "My shoulder's okay, but I've still got a scar where the Mets stuck a knife in my back."

—*Tug McGraw*

"I've never played with a pitcher who tried to hit a batter in the head. Most pitchers are like me. If I'm going to hit somebody, I'm going to aim for bigger parts."

—*Bert Blyleven*

"The first time I ever came into a game there, I got in the bullpen car, and they told me to lock the doors."

—*Mike Flannagan*

This pitcher apparently got tired of being asked trite questions from reporters. Once, after surrendering a home run that cost him a 1-0 defeat, he was asked what it was he had thrown to game hero Tony Conigliaro. The succinct reply was, "It was a baseball."

—*Joe Horlen*

This colorful character was a fine pitcher. His World Series ledger was golden: 6-0 with a 2.86 ERA. When asked to explain his success, he attributed it to "clean living and a fast outfield."

—*Lefty Gomez*

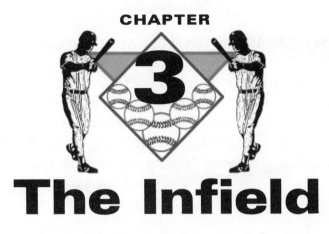

3

The Infield

Fun Facts

Sound Rulings

Umpire Larry Goetz got burned on a "phantom catch" at first base one day. With a runner on second base, Johnny Moore of the Phillies was the batter, and Sam Leslie of the Giants was the first baseman. Moore hit to the shortstop and ran to first base. In the meantime, Goetz watched for the runner's foot to touch the first-base bag. When Moore was two steps from the bag, however, Leslie slapped his glove with his bare hand, and Goetz made the "Out" call.

Moore, who rarely argued with umpires, charged Goetz on this occasion. Goetz, surprised and curious, decided to listen closely to the player's objection.

"Larry, I've got a solid grip," Moore said. "Leslie doesn't even have the ball. They didn't even make the play at first. They made it a third."

Bill Terry, the first baseman for the Giants, was one of the best executioners of the phantom catch. He was a master at stealing an umpire's call.

In the 1933 World Series, he took two clear-cut hits away from the Washington Senators because he knew the habits of the first-base umpire, who watched the runner's foot instead of the fielder's glove. Twice in that series Terry slapped his glove with his bare hand, and twice he got the call from the umpire, who let the sound of the ball hitting the first baseman's glove dictate his call.

'Umpire, Help Me!'

Umpires have been accused of virtually everything from favoring one team over another to trying to end games early. But first baseman George "Catfish" Metkovich of the 1952 Pirates may have been the only player who accused an arbiter of failing to help him play his position.

From the first pitch of a game one hot and sultry afternoon in Pittsburgh, Brooklyn Dodger batters were rifling base hits past Metkovich's head and ricocheting them off his body. Finally, after Duke Snider banked a hard shot off his shins, Metkovich looked at first-base umpire Augie Donatelli and said exasperatingly, "For crying out loud, Augie, don't just stand there. Get a glove and give me a hand."

When a Non-Pitcher Threw a Spitball

You'd expect a spitball to be a saliva-drenched pitch thrown from the mound by, say, a Gaylord Perry. True enough, but once a first baseman was actually guilty of loading up a ball.

The rule book says, "[A] pitcher shall not bring his pitching hand in contact with his mouth or lips while in the 18-foot circle surrounding the pitching rubber." A strange play relating to this rule ensued when Rusty Staub, then playing first base for the Houston Astros, approached the mound to settle down pitcher Larry Dierker.

Staub asked for the ball. Dierker, now the Astros manager, handed it to him. Staub spit on the ball and rubbed it while chatting with Dierker. When he saw Staub applying the drool to the ball, umpire Shag Crawford declared an automatic ball as punishment. Since the count on the hitter was 3-and-1 at the time, Staub caused a walk because he had loaded up the ball!

When a Non-Pitcher
Committed a Balk

In May of 1984, Jerry Remy was playing second base for the Boston Red Sox when he caused a balk. Not only that, he did it without even touching the ball!

Here is how it happened: Marty Castillo of the Detroit Tigers had just doubled. The Sox felt he had missed first base and were about to make an appeal play. Remy thought there was a chance that the Boston pitcher, lefty Bruce Hurst, would overthrow the ball. Since it never hurts to back up a play, Remy positioned himself behind first base in foul ground.

Although the appeal was denied, a strange play resulted. The Tigers requested a balk call because Remy's actions, they argued, violated Rule 4.02, which states that all players other than the catcher must be in fair territory when a ball is in play. The umpires agreed with the Tigers' contention and charged Hurst with a bizarre balk. That's a clear case of an almost-innocent bystander being victimized. Ultimately though, according to the rules, Hurst must take the responsibility.

Hidden Ball, Part I

On September 19, 1997, Matt Williams was playing third base for the Indians against the Kansas City Royals. In the first inning, he decided to try the hidden ball trick. According to Sandy Alomar, "He told the guy [base runner Jed Hansen] to get off the base so he could clean it. He was a rookie. Williams tagged the guy, and he was out. They were pretty upset about that." The Royals were so upset, in fact, that when Williams came to the plate in the next inning, no one was shocked to see him hit by a pitch. Starting pitcher Ricky Bones plunked him with a fastball, nearly starting a fight.

The trick play had actually begun when the Royals' second baseman stole third and began chatting with his third base coach, Rich Dauer. At that point, Williams made his housecleaning request, which the rookie unbelievably obeyed. "I was gullible enough to step off. It took me totally by surprise. I was not paying attention. It won't happen again," said the 25-year-old victim.

Williams explained how the play went: "It was sort of a spur-of-the-moment thing. I wasn't trying to embarrass anyone." Williams had taken the throw on the steal from catcher Pat Borders. He then made a motion as if he were lobbing the ball back to pitcher Brian Anderson. Williams actually tossed the ball into his own glove. His next move was to show the hidden ball to the umpire to alert him as to what was about to happen.

Williams, who had spent his entire career in the National League prior to 1997, was worried, "I've noticed that the umpires in this league call time-out a lot." If the ump had done that, the play would have been dead right there. As it was, Anderson almost blew it by gawking over at Williams.

Coach Goryl marveled, "He did a helluva job with it. That was the first time I saw it done in the big leagues in a long time."

Hidden Ball, Part II

Having succeeded in pulling off the hidden ball trick in 1997, Williams tried it again early in 1998, on April 2—perhaps as a belated April Fools' Day trick. Williams probably picks his targets depending upon their inexperience, since this time he went after 22-year-old Neifi Perez. While Perez technically was not a rookie, he had barely over one-tenth of a year of major league service to his credit.

Perez tripled to lead off the 9th inning for the Colorado Rockies. Williams, by then with Arizona, acted as if he were giving the ball to Diamondback pitcher Felix Rodriguez, who was standing near third base.

Ironically, it was the rookie pitcher who botched the play due to his inexperience. Rodriguez went to the rubber without the ball and was called for a balk.

More Hidden Ball Info

Johnny Goryl said that Tim Ireland, a minor-leaguer, was the best he ever saw at executing this trick. Goryl stated that in one year at the Double-A level, Ireland caught as many as nine guys sleeping. "He was lucky nobody punched his lights out," said Goryl. Ireland would hide the ball by sneaking it under his left armpit. He'd then stand near the runner while jabbing the pocket of his mitt with his fist to lull the runner into believing Ireland did not have the ball. When the runner took a lead, Ireland would retrieve the ball and tag him out.

Another way a fielder once hid the ball was by walking over to the pitcher and plopping the ball into the pitcher's glove. He did this in clear sight of the runner. However, like a magician, he also performed some sleight of hand. Quicker than the eye of the runner could see, the fielder had slipped his own glove inside the pitcher's. Thus, he was actually pounding the ball into his own glove. The pitcher, realizing what was going on, would get off the mound to comply with a rule concerning this trick play. Moments later, another out would be recorded.

Travis Fryman said the trick works because "most players aren't good base runners." He said that if a runner is alert and doesn't stray off a base when the pitcher isn't on the mound, he simply can't get suckered by the hidden ball play. Like many experts, Fryman also feels that Spike Owen was one of the great players at pulling off this trick.

Screen Play

Some tricky third basemen run their own version of a screen play when a runner is at third in a sacrifice-fly situation. Knowing the runner must wait until he sees the outfielder snag the ball before he can tag up, a wily third baseman might purposely get his body in such a position as to block the view of the runner. If the runner can't see the exact moment of the catch, he'll be a second or so slower at leaving the base and, thus, a step or two slower reaching home.

Mike Piazza and the Terminal Tower

Sometimes the cost of player salaries becomes a little too steep, even for a multi-billionaire like Rupert Murdoch. Early in 1998, Mike Piazza, the Dodgers star catcher, demanded a 6-year contract, calling for a cool $100 million. Murdoch declined to offer such an obscene contract as that one, and Piazza eventually wound up with the New York Mets before the '98 season got too far along. The Mets offered Piazza $85 million for six seasons, which added up to just over $14 million per year and would have been the richest baseball contract in history. Piazza felt he was justified in asking for a nine-figure contract because with the 1997 Dodgers he had perhaps the greatest hitting year of any catcher in the history of the diamond game. In 152 games, he averaged a lofty .362, swatted 201 base hits, including 40 homers, and drove in 124.

However, the Dodger organization felt that Piazza, at age 30, would be vulnerable to injury as an everyday catcher, and that he might have a hard time fulfilling the extent of any overblown contract. Piazza was booed throughout the 1998 season by fans in most of the National League for his outrageous salary demands, but he took the jeering in stride as he rolled up another good year, batting .329 in 151 games, with 184 hits, 32 homers, and 111 runs batted in.

$100,000,000 is an enormous amount of money, especially when the sum is considered as a long-term contractual commitment to a baseball player. Consider Cleveland, Ohio, in connection with a massive downtown building project completed in 1930–31. The project featured the Terminal Tower (52 stories and 708 feet high, the second-tallest building in the U.S. outside of New York City), plus four other solid 20-plus–story structures, including the Midland Building. It cost a total of $100,000,000—a massive amount of money in those days. Sure, the dollar is different today than it was two generations ago, but Mike Piazza demanding Terminal Tower money is zany!

Q&A

FIRST BASE

Double Penalty

A Blue Jay runner is on third base with one out when Toronto puts on the squeeze play. The Indian first baseman steals the sign and charges home plate. He catches the pitch before it reaches home plate and applies the tag to the runner five feet up the third-base line.

Legal play?

Answer: No. There is a double penalty on the defensive team: a balk and interference. The runner scores on the balk. The batter is awarded first base on the interference. Rule 6.08 c and 7.07. Both penalties are the result of the first baseman's illegal grab.

Switching Positions

Ernie Banks, who played more than 1,000 games at both shortstop and first base during his major-league career, twists his knee one day while running the bases. His manager, Leo Durocher, doesn't want to remove his star slugger from the game, so he simply switches Banks from shortstop to first base, a less physically demanding position, and changes his first baseman to shortstop.

But the Cubs manager appears to have made a slip: he has forgotten to announce the changes to the umpires.

Does it matter?

Answer: It's an act of common courtesy for the manager who is making the changes to inform the umpire(s) of the switches in the defensive alignment. But players already in the lineup may change positions without informing the umpires. There is no penalty. Rule 3.08 (a—3) and Rule 3.08 b.

A Chancy Play

The first baseman bobbles a hard-hit ground ball, and then, trying to retrieve the loose ball, is run over by the batter-runner in his legal path to the bag. Did the batter-runner interfere with the fielder?

Answer: No. The fielder had a chance to field the ball before the physical contact was made. Rule 2.00— OBSTRUCTION and 7.09 l.

Legal Catch?

Bill Doran of the visiting Astros hits a high, drifting foul pop near the home team's dugout. Cincinnati Reds first baseman Todd Bezinger drifts with the ball, makes a one-hand catch and then, in order to keep from falling, extends his arms to brace himself against the top of the dugout. In doing so, the ball pops out of his glove and bounces into the stands.

Legal catch?

Answer: No. Rule 2.00, CATCH—If a fielder drops the ball as a result of contact with a wall or dugout, it is not a catch.

SECOND BASE

Waiving the Rule

A Red Sox second baseman of recent years, in an attempt to distract a Minnesota Twins batter, positioned himself behind the pitcher and waved his arms frantically while jumping up and down.

Was his act a legal one?

Answer: It was, until Eddie Stanky, the New York Giant second baseman of the early 1950s, employed the tactic one too many times. Because of complaints of his unsportsmanlike conduct, language 4.06 b was inserted in the rule book: No fielder shall take a position in the batter's line of vision, and with deliberate unsportsmanlike intent, act in a manner to distract the batter. The offender shall be removed from the game and shall leave the playing field.

The Red Sox second baseman was removed from the game.

THIRD BASE

The Wind-Blown Ball

Bert Haas of the 1940 Montreal Royals in the International League, Lenny Randle of the 1981 Seattle Mariners, and Kevin Seitzer of the 1987 Kansas City Royals each had one thing in common: they were third basemen who attempted to blow slow-rolling balls foul. They succeeded, except for Seitzer.

By the way, is the play a legal one?

Answer: Well, it was, but it isn't any more. The Haas play was ruled a foul ball. The Jersey City Giants didn't protest the play by Haas or the call by the umpire. Even if they had, there was no rule at the time to cover the play. Shortly thereafter, however, league president Frank Shaughnessy made Haas' play an illegal one.

Larry McCoy, who was the home-plate umpire when Randle made his play, initially ruled the ball foul, but correctly reversed his call. Rule 2.00 OBSTRUCTION.

Line Drive

In a game between the Pirates and the Cardinals, Pittsburgh's Jose Lind hits a vicious line drive that tears third baseman Terry Pendleton's glove off and carries it down the left-field line. Meanwhile, Lind runs the play out to second.

The Cardinals say Pendleton should get credit for a legal catch. The Pirates say that Pendleton threw his glove at the ball, so Lind should get awarded three bases.

What do you think the third-base umpire says?

Answer: The umpire tells Lind to stay at second base. He believes Pendleton's glove came off either accidentally or by the force of Lind's drive. If he thought Pendleton had deliberately thrown his glove at a fair ball, he would award Lind three bases.

Double Jeopardy

The Minnesota Twins have Dan Gladden on second base as Gary Gaetti hits a high hopper between the Chicago White Sox third baseman and shortstop. The third baseman gloves the ball and tries to tag Gladden, advancing from second to third base, but he misses. Then, trying to throw out Gaetti at first base, he hurls the ball wildly into the home team's dugout.

Where do the umpires place Gladden and Gaetti?

Answer: The runners are entitled to two bases from their position at the time of the throw, since the fielder first attempted another play. Gladden, at the time of the throw, had not yet reached third base, so he's entitled to both third base and home plate. Gaetti, at the time of the throw, had not yet reached first base, so he's entitled to both first and second base. Rule 7.05 g.

The Risky Advance

The Reds have Eric Davis on first base with no out. Bo Diaz, the batter, lifts a foul pop toward the Phillie dugout at third base.

Mike Schmidt, the third baseman, drifts with the pop-up and catches it on the playing field, but his momentum carries him into the dugout. Davis tags up and tries to advance to second base, but Schmidt, from the dugout, fires a strike to second baseman Tommy Herr, who applies the tag to Davis for the out.

Answer: Does the umpire-in-chief allow Davis the advance base because Schmidt carried the ball out of play, does he permit the Redleg runner to advance at his own risk, or does he send him back to first base?

Davis advances at risk to himself. Players may enter the dugout to make a catch. Rule 5.10 f.

Missing One Man

The San Francisco Giants and the New York Mets are playing one of their typical twenty-plus-inning curfew beaters. The score is tied 8—8 in the top of the twenty-third inning.

The visiting Giants have a man on first base with one out when their number-four batter hits into a double play. The runner, trying to break up the double play, makes an aggressive slide into second base, and breaks his ankle. The "bad break" is compounded when the Giants can't provide a substitute to take his place at third base in the bottom half of the inning.

Are the Giants allowed to take the field with eight players, or do they have to forfeit the game to the Mets?

Answer: They lose the game by forfeit. Rule 1.01— Baseball is a game between two teams of nine players each. Rule 4.17—A game shall be forfeited to the opposing team when a team is unable or refuses to place nine men on the field.

CATCHERS

The Easy Way?

The Padres, in a game against the Expos, have the bases loaded and two out in the bottom of the sixth inning. Jack Clark is the batter, with a three-two count. On the pay-off delivery by Pascual Perez, the runners break with the pitch. Clark swings and misses. But the catcher drops the ball. Seeing everyone running, he hurriedly picks up the ball and fires it to the first baseman, who drops the ball. All of the Padre runners are safe.

How could the Expos have averted the catastrophe?

Answer: A cardinal rule of baseball is, don't make a throw unless it's necessary. In this instance the catcher simply had to pick up the ball and step on the plate for the force play that would have ended the inning. Rule 6.09 b and 7.08 e.

The Phillies were victimized by this mental and physical error in 1986. An inexperienced Phillies catcher picked up the dropped third strike and threw the ball to first baseman Von Hayes, who proceeded to drop the throw. A run scored and the opposition still had the bases loaded with two out.

Two Gloves?

Rick Dempsey, catcher for the Orioles, decides to experiment one night: he comes out to home plate at the start of the game with his regular catcher's mitt on his left hand and a fielder's glove in his back pocket. He thinks that if he has a play at the plate, he will have a better chance of making it with a fielder's glove than with his catcher's mitt.

The home-plate umpire, who has never seen this done before, asks Dempsey not to carry the extra glove until the arbiter can find a ruling on the situation.

Does the ruling permit Dempsey to carry the extra glove?

Answer: The rule book does not completely cover the situation. It says, however, that there cannot be any equipment left lying on the field, either in fair or in foul territory. That's close enough, the umpires concludes. They tell Dempsey that he cannot use the extra glove.

Clay Dalrymple of the Orioles tested that rule one night in the 1960s against the White Sox. Dalrymple promised the umpire that he would not use the extra glove until a ruling that covered the play could be found, though.

The rule referring to the gloves left on the field implies the offensive team can't leave them. Out of necessity, though, the umpires concluded that the rule also suggested that the defensive team can't leave them, either.

Since that ruling, it's been one glove per player.

Using Mask or Cap

Seattle has Harold Reynolds on second base with Alvin Davis at the plate in a game at Anaheim Stadium. Davis singles to center field, Reynolds rounds third base, and center fielder Devon White throws to the Angel catcher in an attempt to "gun down" Reynolds at the plate. When the catcher sees that Reynolds is going to score easily, and the ball takes a skip hop to his right, he stabs the open side of his mask at the ball, and catches it in the mask. Anything wrong with that?

Answer: The California catcher made a faux pas here. The runner on first base gets three bases. That's right, he scores. A fielder cannot deliberately touch a ball with his cap, mask, or any part of his uniform detached from its proper place on his person. Rule 7.05b.

If an outfielder deliberately touches a fly ball with his cap, the batter-runner is awarded a triple, and he has the option to try to score at his own risk.

Whose Interference?

Pete Reiser, the Dodger runner at third base, sees an opportunity to steal home against the Boston Braves pitcher, who has an extremely slow delivery. But catcher Ernie Lombardi sees "Pistol Pete" break for home out of the corner of his eye, and moves up to catch the pitch and block the plate.

Billy Herman, Brooklyn batter, doesn't realize that Reiser is running, so he swings at the pitch and hits Lombardi. Did Lombardi interfere with Herman's swinging the bat? What does the home-plate umpire do with Reiser? Herman?

Answer: Penalize Lombardi for catcher's interference. Reiser scores and Herman takes first base. Rule 6.08 c— The batter becomes a runner and is entitled to first base without liability to be put out when the catcher or any infielder interferes with him. Reiser scores because of rule 7.04 d: Each runner, other than the batter, may, without liability to be put out, advance one base while he is trying to steal, if the batter is interfered with by the catcher or any other infielder.

Inning-Ending Double Play?

The Pirates have the bases loaded, one out, and Mike LaValliere at bat. He tops a ball in front of the plate, but the topspin on the ball reverses its path, and finally it comes to rest directly on top of home plate.

The Phillie catcher picks the ball off home plate and throws it to first baseman Ricky Jordan for what appears to be an inning-ending double play.

Is it?

Rule 2.00-TAG, 7.08 c—Since the catcher did not make a definite tag of home plate, and since he did not have his foot in contact with home plate when he picked up the ball, it cannot be a force out on the runner from third. So credit only the out at first base, allow the run to score and the other runners to advance on the second out.

Catcher's Balk?

Vince Coleman of the Cardinals is in a steal situation in the late innings, and the Pirate catcher is preparing for the potential theft attempt. While the Pittsburgh pitcher is in the middle of his delivery, the backstop jumps out of the catcher's box so that he will be in a better position to throw out the runner. Coleman runs, the catcher throws him out, and the Cardinals complain. They contend that the backstop committed a catcher's balk. Are they right?

Answer: No, they are not. Rule 4.03 a—The catcher may station himself directly in back of the plate. He may leave his position at any time to catch or make a play, except that when the batter is being given an intentional base on balls, the catcher must stand with both feet within the lines of the catcher's box until the ball leaves the pitcher's hand.

A Hustling Mistake

The visiting Mets lead the Cards in the top half of the sixth inning, 4–0. New York has Rafael Santana on first base, one out, and pitcher Bob Ojeda at bat. It is a bunt situation for the Mets. But pitcher John Tudor gets Ojeda to pop the bunt up behind the plate. The Cardinal catcher springs after the ball and makes a diving effort to catch it, but it just eludes his outstretched glove. It would have been a great play if the catcher had caught the ball.

But would it have been a wise play?

Answer: No. It was a case of good hustle but poor thinking. If the Redbird backstop had caught the ball, he would have been in poor position to throw out Santana, who would have tagged up at first base and advanced to second after the catch. The Cardinals were trying to take away the bunt from the Mets. But in this case the catch would have been as good as a bunt.

Distraction

At the major league level, do managers and players employ tactics that work at the level of American Legion ball? Specifically, if you were a catcher, could you distract an opposing batter by pounding your mitt in an effort to trick him? The batter, hearing the sound coming from the mitt, can tell where the catcher is holding the glove. Presumably, he is telling the pitcher where he wants the pitch thrown.

The reality is that managers don't spend time teaching such tactics, but some players say you can distract or play mind games with your opponent. The story goes that one catcher used to toss dirt and pebbles into a batter's spikes to annoy him. Similarly, Yogi Berra was infamous for making small talk with a hitter in an effort to ruin his concentration. Another example occurred when Hank Aaron responded to Berra's ploys by saying he was in the batter's box to hit, not chatter?

Answer: Mark Grace, an All-Star first baseman with the Chicago Cubs said, "Pounding the glove can work. It can distract you. It puts a thought in your mind. For example, the pitcher went inside with the last pitch, and the catcher is pounding the glove inside again. It can make you think. It's a mind game, but it doesn't stay in the mind too long." With a good hitter like Grace, once the pitch is on the way, such annoyances disappear, and the batter is set to hit.

Grace added that one thing that works for sure, and is quite distracting, is sheer intimidation. "It works for a pitcher," he stated. "That's what chin music is all about. A Nolan Ryan or a Dwight Gooden throws tight and sends a message: Don't dig in!"

INFIELDERS

Unannounced Substitutes

It has been said already that whenever a new player takes a defensive position without notifying the umpire, he becomes an unannounced substitute.

One afternoon in 1970, managers Earl Weaver of the Orioles and Billy Martin of the Tigers found a loophole in the rule, though.

Norm Cash, the first baseman for Detroit, broke the webbing of his glove, and went to the clubhouse to repair it. In infield practice before the start of the following inning, Gates Brown substituted for him at first base. That brought Weaver running out of the Oriole dugout, insisting that Brown had to remain in the game as an unannounced substitute. But umpire Bill Haller permitted Cash to return to his position, saying that what happened in this situation was not the intent of the rule.

In the Orioles' next at bat, catcher Rick Dempsey made the final out of the inning, and went to put on his gear, so Kenny Singleton, the designated-hitter, warmed up the Baltimore pitcher. Then Martin bolted out of the Tiger dugout, demanding, "Singleton's catching. He's an unannounced substitute. He's gotta catch."

Did he?

Answer: The umpires didn't buy Martin's theory, but the following day an asterisk was added to the rules, noting that a designated-hitter may warm up the pitcher without entering the game in the regular catcher's place.

The Infield Fly

Billy and Cal Ripken are on first base and second base, respectively, when a teammate hits a pop fly to the infield with no out.

However, the shortstop loses the ball in the sun, and the ball bounces and hits Cal, who is standing on second base at the time. As soon as the batter hit the ball, he was called out by the umpire on the infield fly rule.

Is Cal Ripken also out? If the infield fly rule had not been declared would he be called out?

Answer: Ripken is safe. Rule 7.08—EXCEPTION: If a runner is touching his base when the infield fly rule is invoked, he is not out, but the batter is out. If no infield fly rule is called, he is called out because he has to advance, since a force play is in effect.

Let's suppose the infield fly rule had not been called. But Cal Ripken, who thought it had been, remains at second base, while Billy Ripken, who knew that it hadn't been, and who saw that the ball was going to drop to the ground cleanly on fair territory, dashes towards second base.

The ball bounces on the infield, caroms off Cal, who is standing on second base, and then strikes Billy, who is approaching second. Double play?

No. Only Cal is out. 7.08 f—PLAY: If two runners are touched by the same fair ball, only the first one is out, because the ball is instantly dead when it touches the first runner.

Let's add one more wrinkle. Suppose, once again, the infield fly rule had been called, and Billy Ripken, who had been running (again), had been touched by the ball.

Double play?

Yes, finally. Rule 7.08 f—If a runner is touched by an infield fly when he is not touching the base, both the batter and the runner touched by the ball are out.

Little-Known Ground Rule

What happens if a fly ball clears a fence that is less than 250 feet from home plate? Although there is a rule prohibiting such a close fence in the major leagues, this could happen at the minor league level.

Answer: Due to an obscure 1926 rule, such a hit is automatically called a ground-rule double.

Legal Strategy?

As a big league manager, would you be allowed to move an outfielder into the infield? Or, could you move an infielder and place him in the outfield?

Answer: Sure, and it has been done. (They say this innovation was created by Branch Rickey.) One day in the 1950s, Charlie Dressen was managing for the Brooklyn Dodgers. Leo Durocher was managing the New York Giants. At one point, Leo "The Lip" pinch-hit for his pitcher. He used Artie Wilson, a player Dressen had managed once in the minors. Realizing Wilson was not a pull hitter, Dressen had his right fielder, Carl Furillo, play between second and third base.

Employing a five-man infield made the left side of the diamond resemble an infield shift, another popular tactic (used mostly against dead-pull hitters such as Ted Williams and Willie Stargell).

Wilson failed to hit the ball into the vacant area in right field, grounding out instead. The gamble had worked, and Dressen looked good.

While managing the Reds, Birdie Tebbetts liked to use the five-man infield in obvious bunt situations.

Recent Five-Man Infield Situations

The Chicago Cubs used the five-man infield as recently as August 8, 1998, against the St. Louis Cardinals. The game was tied in the bottom of the 13th inning with nobody out. There were runners on first and third when Mark McGwire swaggered to the plate. At that point, Cubs manager Jim Riggleman made two decisions.

What were they?

Answer: First, he walked McGwire intentionally to set up the force play at every base—most importantly at home plate. Second, with Ray Lankford at the plate, the Cubs brought center fielder Lance Johnson in to play the infield. Mark Grace remained at first and Mickey Morandini stayed at second. Johnson played between Morandini and the second base bag, giving the Cubs three men on the right side of the infield.

Meanwhile, Sammy Sosa moved over from right to right-center and Henry Rodriguez shifted a bit from left to left-center. Despite all the managerial machinations, the Cubs lost. Lankford, who had struck out his first five times before homering in the 11th inning to keep the Cards alive, singled between Morandini and Johnson to cap a wild 9–8 win.

The Cubs repeated this tactic in a crucial situation during the 1998 season finale. Needing a double play, they brought in outfielder Orlando Merced to play a few feet away from second base. A sacrifice fly made it a moot point in that game.

Swing Shift

Getting back to the more frequently employed infield shift, it was used against San Diego's Greg Vaughn. The Diamondbacks deployed three men on the left side of the diamond in a game on July 22, 1998.

The result?

Answer: Vaughn homered with two men on, giving him his sixth poke in 9 games. It brought to mind the cliché, "You played him deep enough, but not high enough." Vaughn's reaction to the shift was, "I was trying to hit the ball to second base."

Quotations

On his disdain for artificial grass, this slugger commented, "If a horse can't eat it, I don't want to play on it."

—*Dick Allen*

When asked for the highlight of his career, this player responded, " I walked with the bases loaded to drive in the winning run in an intra squad game in spring training."

—*Bob Uecker*

Speaking of his dislike for hitting in Comiskey Park, this player said, "At Wrigley Field, I feel like King Kong. Here, I feel like Donkey Kong®."

—*Gary Gaetti*

Two quotations from an ex-catcher: A) "When Steve [Carlton] and I die, we are going to be buried 60 feet, 6 inches apart." B) On Bob Gibson: "He is the luckiest pitcher I ever saw. He always pitched when the other team didn't score any runs."

—*Tim McCarver*

This Hall-of-Famer said, "So what if I'm ugly. I never saw anyone hit with his face."

—*Yogi Berra*

This West Virginia native wasn't too worldly when he broke into the majors. During his ride to Wrigley Field for his first visit there, he spotted Lake Michigan and asked, "What ocean is that?"

—*John Kruk*

CHAPTER

4

Outfield

Fun Facts

Ken Griffey, Jr. Signs Football Under the Most Unusual Circumstances

Baseball fans often go to unusual lengths to obtain a free autograph from a diamond star, with one of the strangest attempts coming during a Sunday, August 30, 1998 game between the New York Yankees and the Seattle Mariners before a packed house of more than 50,000 screaming fans at Yankee Stadium.

In the bottom of the fifth inning, a fan wearing a number 24 Ken Griffey, Jr. jersey bolted from the grandstand along the left field line directly at the Mariners center fielder. Almost immediately security guards descended upon the interloper from all sides. Griffey stood in place, hands on hips, stunned, unsure of what to expect. "You never know," he said later.

The fan proceeded to hand Griffey a regulation-size football and a pen and asked for an autograph, just before being tackled and heaved to the ground. As the security detail gained control of the fan, Griffey inscribed his signature on the football.

As the fan was hauled away to custody, he stretched out one free hand and Griffey handed him the ball. Alas, the souvenir was later taken away by the tightly disciplined Yankees security contingent.

Ken Griffey, Jr. has always been regarded as "fan friendly." John Sterling and Michael Kay, who were doing the radio broadcast for the Yankees, guffawed throughout the curious incident.

Incidentally, the Mariners thrashed the Yankees 13–3 in that game—and the hitting star for Seattle? Why, none other than Ken Griffey, who smacked two homers and drove in five runs!

Alvin Dark Tells Jim Bouton, 'Take a Hike, Kid.'

Back in 1950, an 11-year-old wide-eyed youngster from Newark, New Jersey, came to New York's Polo Grounds to see the New York Giants in action. After the game, the boy, an avid baseball fan and fledgling autograph collector, stood outside the players' gate in the attempt to snag an autograph or two. Among the first players to emerge was the Giants star shortstop, Alvin Dark. The young fan approached him and said, "Mr. Dark, may I have your autograph?" Dark gave the kid a hard look and said in a gruff manner, "Take a hike, kid, take a hike."

That boy who was rebuffed by Alvin Dark eventually became a big league ballplayer himself, Jim Bouton, who achieved his greatest heights as a 20-game winner for the New York Yankees.

Bouton reported this episode in his best-selling book *Ball Four*, published in 1970. Thus, Alvin Dark's put-down of a young and eager baseball fan became almost universally known. This didn't make Alvin Dark look good, and the incident was all the more incongruous since he was generally held to be a very nice guy in his long career as a star player and big league manager.

We had a chance to speak with Jim Bouton at length at a September 1998 baseball promotional event in New York and asked him if his feelings were really hurt by Dark's refusal to sign his autograph book. Without hesitation, Bouton, now 59 and still looking fit enough to pitch a few innings, replied, "Not at all. I hope I didn't give that impression in *Ball Four*. I was thrilled just by the fact that a noted major leaguer, Alvin Dark, even took the trouble to speak to me, an 11-year-old kid. I actually left the Polo Grounds happy that day!"

When asked about the episode at a 1997 Long Island card show, Dark replied, "I can't remember the incident. After all, it happened more than 45 years ago. Maybe I was just tired that day. I almost always signed if I had the time and if I hadn't been exhausted after playing a game in the hot sun. Remember, I was a shortstop, and that's a very physically demanding position." He went on to emphasize, "I don't want to get a bad rap, because I've always been a guy who's been able to relate to people!"

Alvin Dark has been noted for his abilities as a major league player/manager. One of his ex-players told us, "Alvin Dark was a born leader. I'd run through a brick wall for him." So he didn't sign an autograph for a youthful Jim Bouton. He shouldn't be classed as a villain for that one slight lapse.

Luke Appling Fields a Coffee Pot at Chicago's Comiskey Park!

Luke Appling, the Hall of Fame shortstop, had a big league playing career spanning 20 seasons (1930–1950, with a year out, 1944, for military service) and was known as a great raconteur. He was a baseball "lifer"—he managed and coached a long series of major and minor league teams until his passing at the age of 84 in 1991.

Appling made sports headlines in the summer of 1985, when, at the age of 78, he slammed a home run into the left field stands at Washington, D.C.'s Robert F. Kennedy Stadium during an old-timers' game. Who threw the gopher ball? Why, it was none other than Hall of Famer Warren Spahn, who was a sprightly 64 at the time. After the game Spahn said, "Appling hit the homer on a hanging curve."

About a year after Appling blasted that "senior" home run, we had a chance to interview him at length at a major card show staged in Los Angeles. We asked Luke what was the strangest experience he ever had on a big league baseball diamond.

With only a moment's hesitation Appling replied, "The old Comiskey Park in Chicago was built over a rubbish dump. That means the entire baseball diamond consisted of landfill. In my first full season as a White Sox regular in 1931, we were playing the Detroit Tigers and I think it was the Tigers second baseman, Charley Gehringer, who hit a hot ground ball down to short and I dug deep into the ground in trying to pick up the ball. I didn't come up with the ball, but I did bring up a rusty old coffee pot that had been buried years before the park was completed!

"The next day, the team's ground crew laid down a thick layer of fresh topsoil over the infield so that players at Comiskey could concentrate on picking up baseballs rather than rusty old trash."

Q&A

SHORTSTOP

Ripken's Streak

In 1995, Cal Ripken broke Lou Gherig's record of 2,130 consecutive games. If Ripken had made solely a pinch-running appearance in a game, would that appearance have extended his streak?

Answer: No, it would not. Rule 10.24 c—A pinch-running appearance only shall not extend the streak. On the other hand, a consecutive-game playing streak shall be extended if the player plays one-half inning on defense, or if he completes a time at bat by reaching base or being put out. In addition, if a player is ejected from a game by the umpire before he can comply with the requirements of this rule, his streak shall continue.

Gehrig, by the way, extended his streak several times by either playing one-half inning on defense or completing a time at bat.

Double Occupancy

The Astros have runners on first and second base when Glenn Davis lines a single to left-center field. The runner at second base starts for third base, but he runs into the shortstop in the base path, falls down and then staggers to the sanctuary of third base. In the meantime, the runner at first base rounds second base and coasts into third base without a play.

Two Astros occupy the same base. Pirate third baseman Bobby Bonilla tags the second runner. Is he out? What happens to the first runner?

Answer: The lead runner scores and the subsequent runner remains at third base because of the shortstop's obstruction. Rule 7.06b.

RIGHT FIELD

Error of Judgment

Dave Winfield, the Yankees' right fielder, has a strong arm. An accurate one, too. But once in a while an opposing runner will challenge his throwing prowess. Such was the case in the summer of 1986 when a Kansas City Royals speedster tried to go from first to third on a hard-hit single to right field. Winfield's throw was right on the money, but it hit the sliding runner and bounced down the left-field foul line, allowing the runner to score.

Did Winfield receive an error on the play?

Answer: Yes, he did. A tough one, by the way. He was penalized for making an accurate throw. But if he hadn't been assessed with an error, the pitcher would have been charged with an earned run. Rule 10.13 (e) NOTE. The official scorer is caught in a double dilemma here. Some baseball purists think that in the above situation a team, rather than an individual, error should be ruled.

One night at Yankee Stadium Al Kaline of the Tigers received such an error. He made a great throw and ended up with the game-losing error. But sometimes a pitcher will make the "perfect pitch," and the batter will hit it for the game-winning home run. It is a pitcher's error. These are some of the things which make baseball such an interesting game!

When a Catch Is or Isn't a Catch

In 1991, Triple-A minor leaguer Rodney McCray was roaming the outfield for Louisville. On a long smash, McCray actually ran through a panel of the right field fence near the 369-foot marker. David Justice called this the most amazing thing he had ever seen on a diamond. Justice was in awe of McCray's courage. "At some point he had to know that he had been running for quite a long time." Bone-jarring impact was inevitable.

Clearly McCray made a spectacular catch, hauling the ball in on the dead run under those circumstances. Or did he make the catch? What's the ruling on this play? Is it illegal he caught the ball but left the field of play because of his momentum?

Answer: The rule book states that, in order for a play to be a catch, the fielder has to have complete possession of the ball. In addition, the release of the ball must be voluntary, as opposed to, say, dropping the ball. Had McCray dropped the ball as a result of his impact with the fence, it would not have been a catch. As it was, the catch counted, and McCray became an instant hit on highlight films.

Follow the Bouncing Ball

On May 26, 1993, as Texas was playing the Cleveland Indians, a long fly ball off the bat of Carlos Martinez headed towards Jose Canseco. The not-so-hot-with-the-glove Canseco caught up to the ball, but he didn't catch it. In fact, the ball actually hit him on the head before soaring over the right field fence. Was it a ground-rule double or a homer?

Answer: The umpires that day ruled correctly that it was a (highly embarrassing) home run.

Monday, Monday

On May 10, 1977, the Montreal Expos were at home facing the Los Angles Dodgers. Warren Cromartie tattooed a long drive to center field. Rick Monday gave chase. Although he got close to the ball, it struck the wall over his head. Then it ricocheted off the wall, cracked Monday on his forehead, and rebounded over the wall. Is this play basically the same as Canseco's, or does the fact that it first bounced off the wall change things? What do you award Cromartie?

Answer: Once it hit the wall, it was considered to be a "bounding ball." Such plays result in a ground-rule double, not a home run.

Little League Play

Some plays that work on a lower level of baseball simply don't work at the major league level—or at least they shouldn't work. Still, with the right ingredients, anything goes. For example, on May 12, 1998, the Pittsburgh Pirates were playing the Colorado Rockies. Kirt Manwaring laced a ball into right field for an apparent single. Pittsburgh right fielder Jose Guillen came up with the ball quickly and rifled it to first base. Embarrassingly, Manwaring was gunned out. Later, he likened the experience to the feeling you get in a dream where you run as hard as you can, but you don't move at all.

Why did the play work?

Answer: The play worked because of four factors. First, Manwaring, a catcher, is slow-footed. Second, the ball got to Guillen in a hurry. Third, Guillen fielded the ball quickly, charging in to make the play. Finally, Guillen's arm resembles Roberto Clemente's—it's that good.

LEFT FIELD

Head-First Play

With the bases loaded and one out, Darryl Strawberry of the Mets slices a fly ball down the left-field line at Shea Stadium.

Jerome Walton of the Cubs races from deep left-center field to make a sensational catch, but his momentum forces him to fall head first into the stands.

Is it a dead ball? Can the Mets runners advance at their own risk? Does Walton have to return to the playing field before he can make a subsequent play?

Answer: Rule 5.10 f, 7.04c—The ball is dead when a fielder, after catching a fly ball, falls into the stands or dugout, but each runner is entitled to advance one base.

In Flight?

A lazy fly ball is hit to Phillies left fielder Bob Dernier, but it hits a bird in flight before the Phillie outfielder catches the ball.

Was the ball caught in flight?

Answer: No. (Rule 2.00, Catch In Flight—It is not a legal catch.) The ball remains in play, the batter is safe and can advance at his own risk.

Great Catch Nullified

Back in 1982, Terry Harper of the Atlanta Braves made a great catch that, due to an umpire's call, wasn't a catch. On September 26, in the middle of a pennant race, the Braves were playing the San Diego Padres. In the 3rd inning, San Diego's Gene Richards lofted a ball to left field. Harper speared the ball after making a long run. He caught the ball in fair territory, then crossed into foul territory.

Running as quickly as he was, he needed a good four long strides to slow down. Those strides, though, put him in contact with a low bullpen railing. He grabbed at the railing to brace himself before tumbling into the bullpen area.

Why wasn't it a catch?

Answer: At about that time, he dropped the ball. Now the rule states that a ball that is dropped by a player immediately following contact with a wall is a live ball— no catch has been made. That's why umpire Ed Vargo ruled Harper's play a "no catch," and that's why the speedy Richards was able to cruise around the bases with an inside-the-park home run. To this day, Braves fans feel cheated by Vargo's interpretation that Harper hadn't held on to the ball long enough to validate the catch. They believe that the time that passed from the "catch" in fair territory until Harper hit the fence, including his many long steps holding on to the ball, were sufficient to prove it was a catch. Even an NBA official would've called Harper for traveling on this play, but the ump's call stands, as always.

Sacrificial Players

Imagine that Bernie Williams of the Yankees is at the plate with a runner on third and nobody out. Williams powers the ball to deep left field, where Barry Bonds races for the catch. Realizing the runner from third will easily score on the sacrifice fly, Bonds lets the ball hit his glove, but instead of securing the catch, he begins to bobble the ball. In a weird sort of juggling act, he continues to bounce the ball in and out of his glove while running towards the plate.

When he finally gets to very shallow left field, nearing the shortstop position, he lets the ball settle into his glove. The runner from third knows he can't tag up now, and he stays at third. Is the Bonds trick legal?

Answer: What Bonds did would count as a legal catch. The runner from third, though, was foolish. The rules say you can tag up the moment the ball touches the fielder's glove, not when it is actually caught. If this play really had happened, both the runner and third base coach would have been ripped by the manager and the media as well.

OUTFIELD

The Shoestring Catch

The Mets have runners on first and second base with one out when Tim Teufel hits a short fly ball to right field. Both runners, thinking that the ball will fall safely to the ground, set out for their respective advance bases. But Andre Dawson of the Cubs makes a shoestring catch and throws the ball to first base for an inning-ending double play, just after the runner at second base crosses home plate.

Then the Cubs realize that the run will count unless they appeal the play at second base. But they have crossed the foul line leading to their third-base dugout. They rush back onto the field, and second baseman Ryne Sandberg grabs the game ball and touches second base.

Does the run still count?

Answer: The run counts since the Cubs left the field before they made the appeal. Rule 7.10 d, Paragraph beginning "Appeal Plays"—The defensive team is off the field when the pitcher and all infielders have left fair territory on their way to the bench.

Collision Course

Atlanta Braves left fielder Al Hall and center fielder Dion James are racing for a line drive that has been hit between them. Hall makes a sparkling one-hand grab of the ball, but Jones runs into his teammate, and the collision jars the ball loose from the left fielder's glove.

Is it a legal catch? Suppose the collision had jarred loose both Hall's glove and the ball, which remained in the mitt as it was lying on the ground?

Answer: First, it is an incomplete catch and the ball remains in play. Rule 2.00 CATCH—There is no such thing as a momentarily-held ball. To be a legal catch, the fielder must have firm control of the ball. In either case, Hall didn't. The ball is still in play.

Sac Flies

What is a sac fly?

Answer: Veteran catcher Don Slaught said that if a fly ball is hit to an outfielder when there are fewer than two outs and there is a man on third, "He has to pretend to catch it like he normally does, then basket-catch it. Then if the guy [the runner on third] takes off just a tad too early, maybe we can catch him." If so, it would be a legal play, and the runner would be out for leaving early.

Hondo's Walk

As for a four-man outfield, that is perfectly legal. Dave Bristol is supposed to have used it with Cincinnati in the 1960s.

Frank "Hondo" Howard was always an imposing sight at the plate. He stood 6 feet, 7 inches and went about 255 pounds. The strong outfielder simply scorched the ball. While serving as a coach for Tampa Bay, he reminisced about this unusual managerial move. "I have seen managers with a big power hitter up and a one-run lead going into the 9th inning take one infielder out of the infield and put four outfielders out there. I know Birdie Tebbetts did it to keep away from [giving up] a double."

Why?

Answer: The manager wished to prevent a leadoff two-base hit, since that would put the tying run in scoring position with three cracks still left at knotting the game. He would tolerate a scratch single against his defensive arrangement. Howard was asked who was hitting when Tebbetts made this call, and he replied, "He did it to me."

Another time, Tebbetts placed his shortstop, Roy McMillan, in the outfield to defend against Stan Musial in a situation where Musial's Cardinals needed a long drive to win the game. In that instance, Art Fowler struck out Musial.

Quotations

"Baseball statistics are a lot like a girl in a bikini. They show a lot, but not everything."

—Toby Harrah

During 1998 spring training, this man came to camp over-weight. He joked, "I must have had five coaches come up to me and say, 'I expected to see you floating over the stadium tied to a string . . .'"

—Dante Bichette

"The only reason I don't like playing in the World Series is I can't watch myself play"

—Reggie Jackson

Tired of being reduced to sitting on the bench, and ignoring his lack of productivity, this man said his team was guilty of the "worst betrayal by a team in all sports history. It's not fair to Deion Sanders. It's not fair to teammates or to the fans either. It's one of the worst things ever done to a player." P.S.—His team went on to win the World Series without him.

—Deion Sanders

After fanning in a two-out, potential game-winning situation in the bottom of the 9th inning, this Pittsburgh Pirate of the past lamented, "It's what you dream of right there . . . either you're Billy the Kid or Billy the Goat."

—Glenn Wilson

What player was former pitcher Darold Knowles talking about when he uttered these words: "There isn't enough mustard in the world to cover him?"

—Reggie Jackson

Base Runners

Fun Facts

No-Play

The most exciting play that took place in a game between the 1989 Mets and Giants was a no-play.

Ernie Riles of the Giants was on first base and Kirt Manwaring was the batter with two out. Randy Myers, the relief pitcher for the Mets, stretched, checked the runner, and threw to the plate. Riles broke on the pitch, Manwaring swung at the offering and missed, and catcher Barry Lyons, trying to throw out Riles at second base, threw the ball into center field.

Riles bounced up from his slide and bolted towards third base. Seeing the third-base coach waving him home, he rounded third and raced to home plate. In the meantime, center fielder Lenny Dykstra picked up the errant throw and fired a strike to catcher Lyons, who tagged the sliding Riles for the *fourth* out of the inning.

Manwaring's swing strike was the third out of the inning. But Riles, Lyons, Dykstra, and home-plate umpire Jerry Layne lost track of the number of outs. Sheepishly, Riles said afterwards that he was practicing his base running, Lyons claimed he was practicing his throws to second base, Dysktra contended he was practicing his throws to home plate, and Layne asserted he was practicing his Out call.

Marvelous Marv

One day "Marvelous" Marv Thorneberry of the New York Mets hit an apparent triple, but the opposing team said that the runner missed second base, and they successfully appealed the play. Casey Stengel, manager of the Mets, ran out onto the field to protest the call, but he was stopped by his first-base coach. "Forget it, Casey," the coach said, "he missed first base, too."

Running Wild

Most fans love to watch displays of power. Many fans also enjoy the speed game in baseball. Getting a chance to see a Lou Brock blaze around the bases is a thrill. One of the craziest plays involving speedy runners took place in 1985 when the Chicago Cubs hosted the St. Louis Cardinals.

With Vince Coleman on second and Willie McGee on first, the Cards put on the double steal. Coleman stole third easily, but he ran so rapidly that he slid past the bag. Realizing he couldn't get back to third without being tagged, he jumped up and dashed towards home plate.

Meanwhile, the fleet-footed McGee, who was on second, saw what had occurred and scampered for third. Amazingly, Coleman made it home, and McGee went into third unscathed. The end result was, due to a unique scorer's decision, four stolen bases on one pitch!

An Easy Homer

On July 1, 1997, the Astrodome was the site of yet another crazy play. The Houston Astros were playing the Cleveland Indians. Normally, these two teams would never meet during the regular season because they are in different leagues. However, due to the interleague play that season, they were squaring off.

Each park has its own ground rules, so players need to know the quirks of the ballpark. Not knowing such rules cost the Indians a home run. Manny Ramirez, often accused of having a short attention span, was in right field when a Tim Bogar bouncer rolled down the first base line. Ramirez saw the ball come to rest under the Houston bullpen bench, and he waved to an umpire that the ball was out of play.

The only problem was that the bench was, in fact, in play. First base umpire Charlie Reliford gestured that the ball was still alive. Ramirez's hesitation and lack of knowledge gave Bogar time to circle the bases with an easy inside-the-park home run.

Earl Weaver's Favorite

Outfielder Al Bumbry was a catalyst for manager Earl Weaver for many years with the Baltimore Orioles. Bumbry spoke fondly of a trick play they used to run. With a lefty on the mound and runners on first and third, the Orioles would wait for the pitcher to check the runners.

Bumbry said, "When the pitcher would look back to first, the guy on first would break [or take a big enough lead that he could get picked off on purpose]. When he broke, then the guy on third would break." Since the runner from first went before the pitcher had begun his delivery, the runner appeared to be an easy prey. Thus, the runner from third was often overlooked. When executed properly, the runner from third actually began to run before the pitcher made his pickoff throw to first.

Bumbry smiled. "Earl loved it. We ran it two times in one game against one particular pitcher; it worked. Earl would pick the right spot, and you had to pick the right pitcher, too. There were several elements he'd look for, but generally [the play was used against] one of the nonathletic pitchers, particularly lefties, and a guy who didn't have a very good move. Often it was a big left-hander who had a big delivery to the plate."

Weaver would run it with a righty on the mound, too, but with a slight variation. The runner off first draws a throw, then gets involved in a run down. The key difference here is that the runner from third won't go until the pitcher starts his move to first.

Larry Rothschild, manager of the Tampa Bay Devil Rays, also remembered the play. He said, "Billy Martin did that, too—the 'forced balk,' trying to draw a throw from the pitcher, and then the guy from third scores, or the pitcher balks.

"They do that with a left-hander because [working out of the stretch position] he can see the runner off first [and thus get duped into throwing there]. You're trying to steal home is what you're doing in a different way.

"Sometimes," added Rothschild, "the runner stumbles a little bit [on purpose] so the pitcher really thinks he can pick him off. The second that throw's made, the runner [off third] takes off."

Don Zimmer and the Book

In baseball terminology, if a manager "plays it by the book," he is determining his strategy based on what is considered to be accepted, normal practices. For example, bringing a left-handed relief pitcher into the game in a key situation against a left-handed batter is the usual practice for managers in this oversimplified scenario.

Don Zimmer has built a reputation for being willing to veer away from the routine path on occasion. The gutsy Zimmer has been around the major leagues as a player, coach, and manager since 1954. In 1998, he wore jersey number 50 to celebrate his total of fifty years in organized pro ball. Nicknamed "Popeye" for his facial appearance, he has experienced success at every level of play. In 1996 and 1998, for example, he was Joe Torre's bench coach when the Yankees won the World Series. In 1989, he steered the Cubs to a rare title, capturing the National League's Eastern Division.

Chris Chambliss, a Yankee coach in 1998, said, "As far as somebody who's not afraid to try things, Zim is really the best man to talk to. He's a gambling kind of guy."

Now, your question: Would you, under any circumstances, employ the hit-and-run with the bases loaded?

Most big league managers would probably give you an an emphatic NO! If your name is Zimmer, however, the answer is a qualified yes. If the situation were right, Zimmer would call for the hit-and-run with the bases full.

Since Chambliss said that Zim is the best man to talk to, we did just that. Zimmer explained how and why he pulled such a "crazy" play: "The first time I did it was with Bob Montgomery in Boston. I mean, you've got to have everything right to even think of doing it.

"I happened to have a sinkerball pitcher pitching against us, and Montgomery was a slow runner, but a pretty good bat handler, and I didn't think he could strike

Montgomery out. And I didn't want Montgomery to hit a ground ball because he's slow, and any ground ball that he hit that a fielder could catch is a double play. So it just struck me—play hit-and-run. I did this maybe four or five times in the major leagues."

He seems surprised the play has been so widely discussed. "If you think about it, and when I explain it, it doesn't become that big. You got men on first and second and one out or no outs, and the count goes 3-and-2 on the hitter. Nine out of ten times, the runners are running. Now, extending that logic, why not let three men run with bases loaded?"

Zimmer feels those two plays are similar, so he would hit-and-run with the bases loaded. The advantage is that if the slow-running hitter hits it on the ground versus the sinkerball pitcher, you'll score a run and avoid the double play. On the negative side, a line drive or strikeout can result in a double or triple play, but that's also true of the hit-and-run with first and second occupied. In addition, with the sinkerball pitcher, you're more likely to hit a ground ball than a line drive. So, as Joe Torre said of this play, "With a contact hitter at the plate, why just sit back and wait for the double play?"

Buck Rodgers Concurs

Buck Rodgers, an admiring managerial peer of Zimmer, agreed that the situation would have to include certain favorable factors. Rodgers, who managed against Zimmer in the National League East when he was with the Montreal Expos, pointed out three vital elements: "A batter at the plate who usually makes good contact, a pitcher who has good control and is usually around the plate with his pitches, and a pitcher who isn't a big strikeout pitcher."

Furthermore, the count on the batter would have to be one that would require the pitcher to come in with a strike—a count of 3-and-1, for example.

Dwight Gooden remembered a time Zimmer pulled off this trick: "One year when Zimmer was with the Cubs, with less than two outs, he sent everybody. It was the hit-and-run with the bases loaded. Lloyd McClendon was the hitter. I'd never seen that. It worked," Gooden marveled with a grin.

Such moves don't always pay off, of course. Rafael Palmeiro said, "I remember when [Zimmer] was the manager of the Cubs. I was playing...in '88, and we had the bases loaded in New York against the Mets. Manny Trillo was the batter, and the count was 3-and-2, I believe, when Zimmer put the hit-and-run on. Trillo swung through a pitch up in the zone, and Gary Carter caught the ball and tagged the runner for a double play, and we were out of the inning."

Another longtime baseball man, Johnny Goryl (who once was traded for Zimmer), said, "Zimmer is the kind of a guy who would use [unusual plays] to get an edge on you. Being a student of the game and knowing his players, he would do something like that."

Two More Men's Thoughts

Finally, on the topic of the bases loaded hit-and-run, the thoughts of yet another manager, Larry Rothschild: "I think Don Baylor did it in Colorado a couple of times [this would make sense since Zimmer served as Baylor's bench coach from 1993 to 1995]. You don't see that—the odds of it backfiring and costing you dearly are too great.

"I don't think that's having guts [to run such a play]. I think it's [a matter of] intelligence." Rothschild did concede that it depends on whether a manager such as Baylor has the right situation. "It's more of a calculated risk. If it works, great. If it doesn't, you really screwed up."

Bobby Cox disagrees. "There's nothing wrong with that strategy. Why not try something. I like that type of stuff. There's no 'book.'" He added, "It's a lot more fun." Of course, being with the successful Braves, Cox could afford to try any kind of play.

Sparky's Hit-and-Run

Another legendary manager who employed unorthodox plays at times was Sparky Anderson. Travis Fryman, who played for Anderson, said the only two men he could think of who used unique plays such as a hit-and-run with a man on third were Zimmer and Anderson.

Johnny Goryl said of Anderson, "He'd put on a hit-and-run with a runner on third so the runner could score on a ground ball. The disadvantage is if the hitter misses the ball, you're 'out to lunch,' or you could have a line-drive double play.

"The situation has to be with a contact hitter at the plate who'll put the ball in play on the ground," stated the longtime coach and manager. "Of course the count must also be favorable to the hitter—a count where the pitcher is going to throw a strike."

Frank Howard summed up the play: "What they're really doing is, rather than wait for contact to be made before you start the runner at third base, he's getting his runner in motion in case contact is made on the ground." And, if that contact is made, says Howard, "It's a walk home."

In Theory, That Is

What Howard and Goryl said makes sense, but sometimes a play gets botched. Listen to former Detroit Tiger catcher John Flaherty, who didn't execute the play. "I was playing for Sparky Anderson in 1995, and he put a hit-and-run on with a man on third, a 2-and-1 count, and the infield was in. Of course, I thought I missed the sign, so I stepped out and asked him to go through it again, and they took off the play.

"He let me know after that inning that, for him, all I had to do was put the ball in play and get an easy RBI. So that's why he put the sign on. But I've never seen anybody do that ever before, so it caught me by surprise.

"He did [that play] pretty much with just me, a light-hitting catcher. Just try to put the ball in play—that was the only time it ever came up, though," he observed.

Flaherty was asked if that play is similar to the contact play, and if, with the infield in, it gives the offense a head start with a grounder. He replied, "Exactly. For me, somebody who doesn't run that well and didn't have a lot of power at the time, he thought it was a good opportunity to get an easy run early in the game. But you don't see it very often." Nor, he could have added, will you see it much if players miss the sign because of their incredulity.

Orioles manager Ray Miller has another name to add to the list of innovative managers: "I saw Warren Spahn when he used to manage in the minor leagues. He used to hit-and-run with a man on third all the time. It's not a real envious position for the baserunner coming down the line, and a guy's swinging, but it was different."

Corrales Comments

Ask ten experts about trick plays, and you'll surely get ten different replies. In a 1998 interview, Pat Corrales pretty much agreed with Chris Chambliss: "There aren't too many tricks to baseball other than pickoffs and stuff. The Japanese probably have more tricks than anybody, but a lot of times those things will work more against you than for you. That's the reason we [Atlanta] don't have them." Like Chambliss and the Yankees, who were on a record-setting pace for victories, the Braves, by and large, stick to the basics.

Cheating, Baseball Style

The next trick play calls for speed, guts, and even a wee bit of cheating (which in baseball is sometimes called being crafty). Kevin Stocker described the play: "It's the old double squeeze," he began. "Guys on second and third, and you squeeze bunt and keep the guy from second going. A lot of times we used to run that play [on an amateur level]. I think we may have even done it in the minor leagues.

"When the runners take off on the pitcher, the batter squeezes to the third baseman, and the runner from second cuts the bag at third—he doesn't actually touch the bag. He kinda cuts in front to steal a little time and hopes to catch the umpire sleeping. And it used to work quite a bit. It could work in college, but not so much at this level," he concluded.

The key is that the runner from second never hesitates as the other team goes for the out at first on the bunter. Then, as Stocker says, "You hopefully beat the throw going from first to home." When you succeed here, you get two runs for one little bunt and just one out.

Tagged Out Legally

Frenchy Bordagaray of the depression-starved Dodgers was a good pinch-hitter but a poor base runner. Out of desperation his manager, Casey Stengel, told Bordagaray to stay put once he got on base. One day Frenchy *almost* followed Casey's advice. But he started to hum a song, and then he started to tap the base with his foot when, lo and behold, he got tagged out *in between taps*.

Squeeze Play Notes

In 1969, Johnny Goryl coached in Minnesota with Billy Martin, the last manager who used the safety squeeze to any real extent. Goryl said, "Billy's favorite play was runners at first and third with one out, and he'd have [his hitters such as] Ted Uhlaen-der or Richie Reese drag the ball between the pitcher and the first baseman to steal a run that way.

"And if the first baseman wasn't alert, we might end up with runners on first and second, but it was really to squeeze out a run. It's a weapon to use when you want to add to a lead."

Leyland's Squeeze

Goryl added that nowadays, "Jim Leyland would be one person who would make use of a weapon like that depending on what kind of ball club he's got, where he's at in the batting order and the count, and if the batter's swinging good at the time. All those factors enter into running the squeeze."

More Thoughts on Squeezing

In 1998, a year of tremendous offensive punch in baseball, Scott Brosius offered his view of why squeeze plays aren't used too often. "The way runs are being scored right now, with a lot of the hitters being bigger and stronger, the managers feel that they have a better chance of driving them in from third base instead of bunting them in," said Brosius. "With less than two outs, a lot of the players have a better chance of hitting the ball to the outfield [for a sacrifice fly]."

Chris Chambliss tends to dislike trick plays; he prefers to stick to the basics. He said, "Baseball is a game that does take a lot of doing different things to get your offense rolling sometimes, but we all know what those things are. And you kinda work within your own personnel. If you have guys who hit a lot of home runs, you may not want to be trying all those kind of plays."

The Forward Move

The Minnesota Twins pitcher, who is standing on the rubber, is getting his sign from his catcher when the Kansas City runner on third prematurely breaks toward home plate.

The Twins hurler, who has not yet started his wind-up, breaks directly toward the Royal runner and tags him before he reaches home plate.

Is the runner out?

Answer: Suppose the pitcher had stepped back off the rubber before he chased and tagged the runner.

When the pitcher leaves the mound without backing off the rubber, it is a balk, and the runner is awarded home plate. If he first backs off the rubber, it is a legal play, and the runner is out. Rule 8.01 (a,b,c) and 8.05 a.

In a 1976 game at Shea Stadium, pitching to the Dodgers' Ron Cey, the Mets' Craig Swan committed such a balk.

No Appeal

A Tiger base runner leaves third base early one day on a fly ball to Red Sox center fielder Ellis Burks, but Boston doesn't appeal the play.

Does the umpire make any call?

Answer: No appeal, no call. Rule 7.10 (a).

Stan Musial of the Cardinals did that one day. Richie Ashburn was in center field for the Phillies. Musial left third base before the ball touched Ashburn's glove. But Willie Jones, the Phillies third baseman, didn't call for an appeal. The run counted.

On the other hand, Smoky Burgess, who could hit but couldn't run, was notorious for leaving third base a split second too soon on a tag-up play. But opposing teams had a standard rule for Burgess—automatic appeal. And, more often than not, the run wouldn't count.

Caught Without the Ball

The Braves and the Phillies are scoreless in the seventh inning. Atlanta has Dale Murphy on third base with one out. On a ball that is hit back to the mound, he gets caught off third base, and a run-down ensues. As the Phillies third baseman and catcher exchange throws, the pitcher gets positioned in between the runner and the ball. Murphy, in trying to avoid being tagged out, runs over the pitcher.

Is there any call?

Answer: Yes, the runner is entitled to the advance base, in this case home plate. Rule 7.06 a.

This play happens every once in a while on a baseball field. For example, the visiting Indians and the Senators were scoreless in the eighth inning of a 1949 game. Eddie Robinson was the runner at third base. Early Wynn was the pitcher. As soon as contact was made, the umpire said to Robinson, "You score."

One of the intriguing things about that play is that Cleveland Indian manager Lou Boudreau was not aware that the obstruction rule existed, so he argued the call strenuously. The next day, he apologized to the umpires and told them they had made the right call.

The Step and Tag Play

Dave Winfield of the Yankees singles with one out in the top of the ninth inning. Don Mattingly, who follows him in the lineup, smacks a ringing line drive toward Blue Jay first baseman Willie Upshaw.

Winfield, thinking that the ball will be caught on the fly by Upshaw, retreats to first base. In fact, Upshaw fields the ball on a short hop, and Winfield, knowing that he cannot safely reach second base, remains on first base. Upshaw first steps on the bag and then tags Winfield.

Is it an inning-ending double play?

Answer: No. Mattingly is out and Winfield is safe. As soon as Upshaw stepped on first base, he removed the force on Winfield. If Upshaw had tagged Winfield before touching the base, it would have been an inning-ending double play. Rule 7.08 e.

This play occurred in the top of the ninth inning of the seventh game of the 1960 World Series. Mickey Mantle of the Yankees was on first base, and Yogi Berra was the batter who hit the ball. Rocky Nelson of the Pirates was the first baseman. Asked afterwards why he didn't tag Mantle before he touched the base, he said, "They don't call me Rocky for nothing."

In the bottom of the ninth inning, Pirate Bill Mazeroski's game-winning, Series-winning home run made Nelson's choice academic.

The Tricky Tag

Rickey Henderson is the Oakland A's runner at third base. There is one out in the bottom of the ninth inning of a 3–3 game. Jose Canseco, the batter, hits a medium-distance fly ball to Red Sox left fielder Jim Rice. In the meantime, Henderson backs up several yards behind the third-base bag in order to get a running start by the time the ball is caught. Just as Rice catches the ball, Henderson hits the bag in full stride and goes on to score easily.

Do the A's win?

Answer: Not if any of the Red Sox tag third base and make an appeal to the umpire who is assigned to that position. Rule 7. 10a—A running start is illegal on a tag-up play.

Until the early 1950s Henderson's play used to be a legal one. But shortstop Alvin Dark of the New York Giants used the play to his and his team's advantage so often that the rules inserted 7.10 a to eliminate the loophole.

Fielder's Choice

Kirby Puckett of the Twins, thinking of stealing second base, anticipates Milwaukee pitcher Juan Nieves' move and gets a good jump toward second. But Nieves throws to first base instead of second base. Puckett never breaks stride, however, and slides into second base safely as Milwaukee's first baseman throws the ball wildly into left field.

Does Puckett get a stolen base on the play?

Answer: No, he does not. Rule 10.08 f. If he had made it safely to second base without the aid of this error, or any high or wide throw, he would have received a stolen base. Had he been thrown out, it would have been an attempted steal.

Darryl Strawberry of the Mets was picked off first base on such a play during the 1986 season. The Phillies first baseman, however, threw the ball away. Strawberry didn't get a stolen base. It was ruled an error on the first baseman and a fielder's choice.

A Picky Play

A Seattle Mariners runner steals second base successfully, but in getting to his feet, he lifts his foot off the bag, and the Oakland A's second baseman applies the tag to him. Will the umpire call the runner out in this instance, or will he invoke the "neighborhood play?"

Answer: The neighborhood play was made popular by Gil Hodges. If any first baseman or infielder had his foot in the neighborhood of the bag when he caught a throw, the umpire would consider it close enough, and it did not actually have to be in contact with the bag. In that way, it avoided a lot of injured toes and feet.

The umpire will call the runner out, but it will probably create a rhubarb. Rule 7.08 c. At least it did the day umpire Beans Reardon called Charlie Pick of the Cubs out on the play. First, Reardon called Pick out. Then, when the runner argued too vociferously about the call, the umpire threw him out of the game. Finally, when the Bruin outfielder responded too physically, Reardon "punched him out."

Successful Steal?

In a game at Veteran's Stadium in Philadelphia, the Cardinals had Ozzie Smith on second base and Gene Tenace on first base with two out, when the Redbirds attempted a double steal. Catcher Bob Boone of the Phillies, realizing that he had no play on Smith at third base, threw to shortstop Larry Bowa to retire the follow-up runner at second base.

Did Smith receive credit for a steal?

Answer: No, he did not. Rule 10.08 d—When a double or triple steal is attempted and one runner is thrown out before reaching and holding the base he is attempting to steal, no other runner shall be credited with a stolen base.

Breaking the Tie

In a game between Los Angeles and host Cincinnati, the Dodgers second baseman is called out at first base on a bang-bang play. But the Dodgers contend that there was a tie between the runner's foot hitting the bag and the fielder's throw hitting the first baseman's glove. Tie goes to the runner, they say. The umpire agrees there was a tie, but disagrees with their interpretation of the rule. He calls the runner out.

Who is right?

Answer: The umpire is right. Some rule books do say that a "tie goes to the runner." But not the major-league rule book. There's no mention of a tie, in face. The runner either beats the throw or he doesn't. In this case, he didn't.

Steve Sax of the Dodgers was thus "victimized" in a real game. The play happens just about every day of the year on a big-league diamond.

A Steal or Not a Steal?

Walter "Boom Boom" Beck of the Phillies, forgetting that he has a runner on second base, goes into his wind-up rather than the stretch.

Frenchy Bordagaray, the Cardinal runner, gets a good jump and reaches third base before Chick Hafey, the batter, pops the pitch up to the second baseman. Bordagaray, thinking that he had legally stolen third base, makes no effort to return to second base. The second baseman flips the ball to the shortstop, who is at the bag, for the double play.

Should the runner have tried to return to second base?

Answer: Yes, because otherwise he is out, even though he reached third base before the ball was put in play (Rule 7.10 a).

Umpire's Interference

A Blue Jays infielder drills a fastball off the right-center-field fence and is legging out an apparent triple. But he runs into an umpire who is stationed in the base path between second and third base. The Toronto player falls to the ground, gets up groggily, and stumbles into the third baseman's tag.

Is the runner entitled to third base?

Rule 2.00—INTERFERENCE (c)—When a runner collides with an umpire, it doesn't constitute interference, and the ball remains in play.

The Blue Jay in the above situation is out. He is supposed to avoid hitting an umpire.

Unintentional Interference

A Houston Astros runner takes a lead off first base as the batter hits a hard one-hopper to Atlanta Braves first baseman Gerald Perry.

The runner, thinking that Perry will remove the force play by first stepping on the base, makes a false start for second base, then reverses himself and slides back into first base. But Perry throws to second baseman Ron Gant for the force play, and the pivot man's return throw to Perry bounces off the sliding runner, allowing the batter-runner to reach first base safely.

A man who has already been forced out can't interfere with a follow-up play. Can he?

Answer: The unintentional interference is not illegal, so the batter-runner is safe. Rule 7.09 f—If the batter or runner continues to advance—forward or backward to a base—after he has been put out, he shall not by that act alone be considered as confusing, hindering, or impeding the fielders.

The Two-Out Fly Ball

The Pirates have Barry Bonds on third base and Bobby Bonilla on first base with one out when Andy Van Slyke flies out deep to the right-center-field fence. Bonds scores easily after the catch, but Bonilla, thinking that the ball is going to fall safely for a hit, rounds second base before the catch is made. He retraces his steps but is thrown out before he reaches first base.

Does the run that Bonds scored count?

Answer: The run counts. This is not a force play, although the runner must return to first base. Rule 4.09 a—In the above situation, all the runners can score, if possible.

Protected by Being on Base?

Dave Magadan of the Mets takes a walking lead off third base in foul territory. Kevin McReynolds hits a hard ground ball in the base runner's direction. Magadan instinctively retreats to the sanctuary of the base, but he is hit by the batted ball in front of the third baseman.

Does the possession of the base protect Magadan from liability to be put out?

Answer: Rule 7.08 f—The base does not protect the runner when he is hit by a fair batted ball before it has passed an infielder. If Magadan had been in foul territory when he was hit by the ball, it would have been a foul ball, and he would have been safe. But he was hit by the ball in fair territory before it had passed an infielder, so he was out.

Batter's Interference

Paul Molitor of the Brewers is on third base with one out. The Oakland pitcher takes a slow wind-up, so the Milwaukee infielder decides to steal home. The batter takes the pitch, but his subsequent move illegally screens the catcher off the play, allowing the runner to cross the plate.

Someone has got to be called out for interference. Who? Would it make any difference if there were two out?

Answer: Rule 6.06 c and 7.08 g—With less than two out the runner is called out; with two out the batter is ruled out. Neither way is the run allowed. In this particular play Molitor would be called out.

Removing the Force

The California Angels have Wally Joyner at third base, Johnny Ray at first base, two out, and their number-four man in the lineup at the plate with a three–two count. The batter grounds to the shortstop, who juggles the ball, then tosses it to the second baseman too late to force the sliding Ray. But Ray, just slightly after Joyner crosses home plate, overslides the base and is tagged out by the second baseman. Does the run count?

Answer: Yes. Rule 4.09 a and 7.08 e—Ray's touching second base removed the force play. After oversliding the base, he had to be tagged in order to be retired. Joyner's run counts.

Ball Enters Dugout

The Tigers' Lou Whitaker is on first base when Alan Trammell smashes what appears to be a sure extra-base hit to left-center field. Whitaker rounds second and is headed toward third base when Indian left fielder Joe Carter makes a spectacular one-hand running catch. Whitaker retraces his steps and is approaching first base when the shortstop's relay throw gets away from the first baseman and rolls into the dugout.

Where does Whitaker finally wind up?

Answer: Rule 7.05 g—Whitaker is placed at third base. He is considered to be on first base because that is the base he will and must retouch before legally advancing. Two bases are awarded when the ball goes into the dugout.

Fair Game

Jack Clark of the Giants, with no out in the bottom of ninth inning of a tie game, doubles to left and advances to third base on a ground ball out to second base. The Mets, hoping to throw out the potential winning run at the plate, play both their infield and their outfield shallow. Kevin Mitchell then drives a solid smash past third baseman Howard Johnson. The ball strikes Clark, who is standing in fair territory, and caroms down the left-field line in foul territory. Clark proceeds to hobble home with the winning run.

Is he safe or out?

Answer: Rule 7.08 f—Any runner is out when he is touched by a fair ball in fair territory *before* the ball has touched or passed an infielder, and if no other infielder has made a play on the ball. Because Johnson was in front of Clark when the ball passed him, the runner is safe. The Giants win.

Courtesy Runner

Joe Carter of the Indians doubles to open up the top half of the second inning, but he sprains his ankle on his slide into second base. The game with the Red Sox is for first place, though, so Carter wants to remain in the game. In order to do so, however, he knows that he will have to get his ankle wrapped. He requests a courtesy runner and the right to return to the game in the bottom half of the inning.

Can he do that?

Answer: Up until 1950 he would have been able to do it. Now, once removed from the game, a player may not re-enter, no matter what the circumstances. Rule 3.03 and 3.04.

Juggle Ball

Robin Yount of the Brewers is on third base with no out when Rob Deer hits a long fly ball to right field.

Mel Hall of the Yankees reaches for the ball, deflects it into the air, juggles it a few times, and finally catches it.

Yount tags up at third base and leaves the bag as soon as Hall touches the ball for the first time, and he trots home easily with the run. But the Yankees, claiming that Yount left third base too soon, appeal the play at third.

Do they get a second out?

Answer: No, they don't. Rule 2.00, A CATCH—A runner may tag up and leave the bag the instant a defensive player touches the ball. A catch is legal if the ball is finally held by any other fielder, even though juggled, or held by another fielder before it touches the ground.

The Comebacker

With Ryne Sandberg of the Cubs on second base with one out, the next batter strikes out, and heads directly toward his dugout on the first-base side of the field. But the opposing catcher has dropped the pitch. Suddenly Sandberg bolts toward third base, and Angel pitcher Mike Witt, now with the ball back from the catcher, throws him out. When the Chicago batter-runner, who is about ten feet from his dugout, sees that Witt's throw is to third base, he turns and sprints toward first base.

In the meantime, the third baseman after tagging Sandberg, throws the ball high over the first baseman's head. By the time the ball is retrieved and returned to the infield by the right fielder, the Cub runner is standing on third base.

Do the umpires permit him to stay there?

Answer: Yes. The entire play is legal. The key to the play is that the runner did not enter the dugout. Rule 7.08, APPROVED RULING.

Three-Run Triple Single

The Indians have the bases loaded with two out when their clean-up batter hits a ball off the wall good for three bases. Running out his hit, however, he misses touching second base. The second baseman notices the runner's oversight, calls for the ball, and makes a successful appeal.

Since it's the third out, do the runs count?

Answer: Rule 4.09 a, 7.02, 7.10 b—The third out on the appeal did not occur until after the three Indian runners had scored, so the runs count. The batter, however, winds up with only a single.

Tape-Measure Home Run

Mickey Mantle hit so many tape-measure home runs that not even he can remember all of them.

One afternoon at Sportsman's Park in St. Louis, he hit one almost out of the state of Missouri. There was a runner on second base and one out at the time. When Mantle hit the ball, the runner, who was approaching third base, glanced over his shoulder to see where the ball was going to land. In doing so, he missed touching third base en route to home plate.

The Browns appealed the play at third base, and the umpire called the runner who missed the base out. But what about Mantle? Did he have to return to second base? Or was he out for passing the last legally touched base?

Answer: Mantle got credit for a home run. Rule 7.12— Unless two are out, the status of a following runner is not affected by a preceding runner's failure to touch or retouch a base.

Attempted (?) Steals

Rickey Henderson is an aggressive base runner. That is one of the reasons that he stole a record 130 bases in 1982. It is also one of the reasons that he was thrown out attempting to steal a record 42 times in 1982. Anticipating the pitcher's move to the plate, Henderson likes to take a walking lead to the advance base.

Let's consider three possibilities. First, Rickey is picked off while trying to return directly to the base that he left. Is the out recorded as an attempted steal?

Answer: No.

Second, he is picked off but he eludes a rundown and slides safely into the advance base. Is he credited with a steal?

Yes.

Third, he is picked off and tagged out while trying to reach the advance base. Is the out recorded as an attempted steal?

Yes.

The second situation is covered by rule 10.08 c: When a runner, attempting to steal, or after being picked off a base, evades being put out in a rundown play, and advances to the next base without the aid of an error, credit the runner with a stolen base.

The third situation is covered by rule 10.08 h (2): A runner shall be charged with "caught stealing" if he is put out, or would have been put out by errorless play when he is picked off a base and tries to advance—any move toward the next base shall be considered an attempt to advance.

You Can't Go Home Again

With two out Chet Lemon of the Tigers triples with the bases loaded. But the runner on third misses touching home plate. After the runners from second and first base score, he goes back to home plate to retouch it. The catcher then calls for the ball and appeals the first runner's miss of home plate.

Should the umpire uphold the appeal?

Answer: Yes. Rule 7.10 b—APPROVED RULING, 7.12—The runner cannot return to touch a base after succeeding runners have touched it. In this case it represents the third out, so no runs score.

Stealing Home

Rod Carew stole home a record-tying seven times in one season.

In this hypothetical situation he is on third base and teammate Harmon Killebrew is on first base. Carew gets a big lead, flashes the double-steal sign to Killebrew, and breaks for home on the pitcher's wind-up. He crosses the plate safely before the pitch hits him in the strike zone. Killebrew, in the meantime, misses Carew's sign, but advances to second base when the bounding ball bounces toward the first-base dugout.

Is Carew out for being hit with the pitch? Is the pitch a strike? Is Killebrew allowed to advance to second base?

Answer: Carew is safe since he touched home plate before he was hit with the pitch. The plate umpire calls the pitch a strike since it was in the strike zone. If there were two strikes on the batter before the pitch, the hitter would be called out. If there were two out before a two-strike pitch, the inning would be over, but the run would still count, because it scored before the out was called. In addition, Killebrew is allowed to remain at second base because of Rule 5.09 h: Runner(s) may advance if any legal pitch touches a runner trying to score.

Slip in the Mud

The Orioles' Billy Ripken and Cal Ripken break from second and first base, respectively, as Mickey Tettleton hits an extra-base hit to the wall.

Both runners would normally score easily, but Billy slips in the mud halfway between third base and home plate. Cal comes up behind Billy, helps him to his feet, and without passing his brother, pushes him in the direction of home plate. The two of them cross home plate just before the relay throw reaches the catcher.

Legal play?

Answer: Yes—there is no penalty in the above situation. Rule 7.09 i—When a runner helps a teammate, there is no penalty. If a coach physically helps a runner, however, there is a penalty.

Checked Calls

Don Mattingly of the Yankees is on third base with two out and a two-two count on Dave Winfield. Teddy Higuera of the Brewers breaks off a hard-breaking curve ball that bounces in the dirt. Winfield appears to check his swing as the ball eludes Milwaukee Brewer catcher B.J. Surhoff and bounces back to the screen. In fact, the home-plate umpire calls the pitch a ball.

On the play, however, an alert Mattingly scores. An equally alert Surhoff appeals Winfield's checked swing to the first-base umpire, who rules that Winfield had indeed swung at the pitch. Surhoff then tags Winfield for the third out.

Does Mattingly's run count?

Answer: The run does not count. Rule 4.09 a, EXCEPTION—A run is not scored if the runner advances to home plate during a play in which the third out is made by the batter-runner before he reaches first base.

Dave Winfield's checked-swing call reminiscent of other conflicting calls.

Ron Northey of the Cardinals once got tagged out at home plate at the end of his home-run trot. He had thought the ball he had hit was a home run. With good reason. A base umpire had flashed him the home run sign. But another arbiter had called the ball "in play." The protest that followed was upheld, and the game was replayed from that point.

Gus Bell of the Pirates once let two Cardinals runners score because he had seen third-base umpire Babe Pinelli rule his catch the third out of the inning. However, he had not seen second-base umpire Bill Stewart rule his play a trapped ball. Stewart was closer to the play, so his call stood.

Umpire Al Barlick once ruled a diving attempt by Andy Pafko of the Braves a trapped ball. Pafko was so sure that he had caught the ball on the fly that he ran directly to Barlick to argue the play. In the meantime, Rocky Nelson of the Cardinals circled the bases with one of the strangest inside-the-park home runs in major-league history.

Entrapment?

The Cardinals have one out, Vince Coleman on third base, Willie McGee on first base, and a rookie who is trying to make the St. Louis ball club at the plate. Zane Smith is pitching in relief for the Braves.

The rookie hits a high fly ball to short right field where Dale Murphy, who has noted that the batter-runner has stopped running midway on his path from home plate to first base, lets the ball drop at his feet. He then picks up the ball and fires it to first baseman Gerald Perry, who first tags McGee, who is standing on first, and then steps on the bag.

One out? Double play? Entrapment? Suppose Coleman had tagged up at third base and scored before the third out was made?

Answer: Double play. Rule 6.051 1—APPROVED RULING and 7.08 e. There was entrapment. But it was the rookie who entrapped himself. If he had run out the play, Murphy's deception wouldn't have worked.

Coleman's run would not count. A runner cannot score on a force double play that ends an inning. Also, he can't score when the batter-runner makes the third out of an inning at first base.

Instant Ejection

A Kansas City player who is still seething over two close plays on potential base hits that went against him earlier in the game hits a home run in the eighth inning and proceeds to give the umpire at first base a mouthful of abuse as he rounds the bag. The umpire immediately ejects the runner.

Is the batter-runner out of the game as of that moment, or can he legally complete his home-run trip before he has to leave the premises?

Answer: The Royals runner is allowed to complete the play. Then he must leave the playing field. Rule 9.01 d—If an umpire disqualifies a player while a play is in progress, the disqualification shall not take effect until no further action is possible in that play.

Live-Ball Emergency

Willie Randolph has been plagued by leg problems during the twilight years of his career. Let us say that the second baseman hits an apparent double to the left-center-field wall, but in running out his hit, he suffers a hamstring muscle pull between first and second base, and can't complete his route.

Can a pinch-runner complete Randolph's course?

Answer: No. A pinch-runner can't be inserted, because the ball is live. Rule 5.10 e-1 says that if an accident to a runner is such as to prevent him from proceeding to a base to which he is entitled, that is, an award of one or more bases, a substitute runner shall be allowed to complete the play. Randolph wasn't "entitled" to two bases on the play. If the hit had been a ground-rule double, he would have been.

The 'Smart' Runner

Let us say that the visiting Red Sox have the bases loaded with no one out in a game against the Rangers. Dwight Evans is on third base, Marty Barrett is on second base, and Wade Boggs is on first base when Mike Greenwell hits a hard ground ball right at the shortstop.

Barrett, realizing that the ball represents a tailor-made double play, deliberately lets the ball hit him, thinking that one out is better than the probable two.

You're the second-base umpire. What's your call?

Answer: If you think that Barrett intentionally interfered with the ball, you call him out and you have to call out the batter-runner, Greenwell, too. Rule 7.09 g.

Ron Luciano, the umpire, once made that call against Texas Ranger shortstop Toby Harrah. A heated argument followed, but Luciano prevailed, of course.

Jackie Robinson, the shrewd second baseman for the Brooklyn Dodgers, got away with that play several times in his major-league career, on the other hand.

Getting the Drop on Him

The Mets have a runner on first base and one out in a game against the Cubs. Tim Teufel then lines a drive right at the Cub third baseman, who deliberately drops the ball, picks it up and throws to second baseman Ryne Sandberg, who pivots and fires to first baseman Mark Grace for an inning-ending double play. Does the play stand as the Cub third baseman designed it?

Answer: No. The rules protect the runner from this vulnerable situation. Rule 6.05 l—The batter is declared out, the ball is dead, and the runner(s) may not advance.

Three Bases Only?

Von Hayes of the Phillies hits a line drive between the Astros' right and center fielders. In frustration the right fielder throws his glove at the ball and nicks it before it rolls to the wall. Hayes, circling the bases, tries for an inside-the-park home run. But the relay from center fielder Gerald Young to second baseman Bill Doran to catcher Alan Ashby nips Hayes at the plate.

Phillies manager Nick Leyva argues, however, that Hayes should be entitled to return to third base because the thrown glove hit the ball. Is Leyva right?

Answer: No. Because the thrown glove hit the ball, Hayes *was* entitled to three bases, but he tried for four bases. On such a play the ball remains in play, and the runner at risk to himself tried to score. Rule 7.05 c.

He Can't Return Again

The Red Sox have a runner on first base when Dwight Evans hits a long fly ball to left-center field. The runner, thinking that the ball will hit the wall, rounds second base, but then retreats quickly when Kansas City Royal left fielder Bo Jackson makes a sensational diving catch.

In his rush to return to first base, the runner misses touching second base. In the meantime, Jackson throws the ball to the shortstop, whose relay throw to first base goes into the dugout.

What happens to the runner?

Answer: The runner, on the throw into the dugout, is entitled to third base. Once the ball is dead, however, he cannot return to touch a missed base after advancing to and touching a bag beyond the missed base. An appeal in this instance would be valid. As soon as the ball is put in play, the defensive team has the right of appeal. If it fails to do so, however, the runner remains at third base. Rule 7.02 and 7.05 g.

Double Interference

The San Francisco Giants have runners on second and third base with two out when the batter hits a high-hopper towards the hole between third base and shortstop. The Los Angeles Dodger third baseman cuts in front of the shortstop and just as he gloves the ball, the runner who had been on second base runs into the shortstop, who was in the base path. The third baseman then drops the ball and all runners reach their advance base safely.

Or do they?

Answer: All runners are safe. The inning continues and the run counts. Only one fielder is entitled to the right of the interference rule. Since the third baseman actually fielded the ball, the runner's contact with the shortstop is incidental. Rule 7.09 l.

Blocking the Plate

Tim Raines of the Expos is on second base when Hubie Brooks lines a single to center field. Raines tries to score on the play, but he slides into the Cincinnati Reds catcher, three feet from home plate, before the ball skips by the receiver.

Pitcher Tom Browning, who was backing up the catcher on the throw from the outfield, retrieves the ball and throws it to first baseman Barry Larkin, who is covering the plate. He tags Raines before he can touch the plate. In the meantime, Brooks advances to second base.

Does the play stand?

Answer: No. Obstruction is called on the catcher for blocking the runner without possession of the ball. The run scores and the subsequent action is inconsequential since the ball is dead. Brooks is returned to first base. Rule 7.06 a.

After the Fact

The Orioles have runners on second and third base with two out when Mickey Tettleton hits a long fly ball to the outfield. The runner from third base tags up and scores easily, and the runner from second base tags up and advances to third base. But the second baseman for the Texas Rangers claims that the runner at second base left the bag too soon, and the umpire, upon appeal, agrees with him. The runner is called out.

Does the run count?

Answer: The run scored before the third out, so it counts, because the final out of the inning was not a force out. Rule 4.09 a.

Haste Makes Waste

The Pirates have runners on second and third with one out when Barry Bonds hits a medium-distance fly ball to Montreal Expo left fielder Tim Raines. The runner on third base, in his haste to score, leaves the bag before Raines makes the catch. On Raines's throw to the plate, however, the ball gets away from the Expo catcher, and both runners score.

The Pirates make an appeal on the first runner, who left third base early, and get the third out of the inning.

Does it nullify the follow-up runner's score?

Answer: Yes. Since the play results in the third out, the appeal retires the side, and the run doesn't count. If it had resulted in the second, rather than the third, out, the follow-up runner would not be affected, and his run would count. Rules 7.10 a and 7.12.

Prevent the Squeeze?

If the runner on third tips off the squeeze play, would a manager ever have the pitcher deliberately hit the batter? By hitting the batter, the ball is dead, and the runner must return to third. Would a manager advocate this?

Answer: It depends on whom you listen to, but we think he would. Stocker said, "They're not going to throw at you to hit you; they're going to throw it high and tight or up and away—trying to get you to foul it off. They might try to throw it in the dirt.

"The goal is not so much to try to hit you or get an out. The goal is to try to get you to bunt it foul or miss the ball," he concluded. Of course if you miss the ball, the result is an out. If you pitch the batter high, and he bunts a pop-up, you could get a double play.

Now, if you ask Bobby Cox if you should hit a batter, he'd reply, "I think you would at least throw it at him."

He also said the other option was to throw it way outside. "You'll do one or the other if you smell it—if he's coming way down the line too early. You'd better do it [hit him] to save a game. If you read it, you've got to adjust. You're not going to hurt anybody, I'm just saying, to stop the play you damn near gotta do it."

He said that to come in "high and tight is what you should do, knock him down, and the catcher's got the ball. If it hits him, it hits him." He viewed such a tactic as being, in effect, "the same thing as a pitchout."

CHAPTER

From the Dugout

Fun Facts

Roasting the Umpire

Figuring out who are the strident bench jockeys is sometimes a difficult job for an umpire. Once in a while he will go by a player's reputation. On occasion he will base his decision upon instinct. Working a Giants-Dodgers game at Ebbets Field one day, home-plate umpire Tom Gorman was getting roasted by the Brooklyn bench. Finally he had endured enough and decided to retaliate on the basis of reputation and instinct. "Van Cuyk, you're through for the day," he said as he charged the Dodgers dugout. "Get out of here!"

No one on the bench moved.

"Come on, [Chris] Van Cuyk, get moving. Go take a shower."

Still, there was no movement. Gorman then angrily turned toward manager Chuck Dressen and said, "You better get him out of here. If you don't, I'm going to clear the whole bench."

Dressen got the last laugh that time, though. "If you want to thumb Van Cuyk, you'll have to go to St. Paul, 'cause that's where I sent him yesterday."

Eight-Inning Game?

Some players lose track of the number of innings in a game. Take Jim Corsi of the 1989 Oakland A's, for example. Brought up from Tacoma just before a game with the New York Yankees, he was understandably excited. So when Rick Honeycutt of the A's got the final out of the eighth inning, Corsi was the first Oakland player out of the dugout to congratulate the relief pitcher on his victory. Also the only one.

Honeycutt, who was both confused and amused, looked at the rookie and said, "They play only eight innings in Tacoma?"

An inning later, Honeycutt got the final out of the game.

Batboy Gets Thrown Out of a Game for Stealing Signals

Bert Padell today operates one of the nation's largest financial management agencies for show business and sports celebrities. His firm, Padell, Nadell, Fine, Weinberger & Co., occupies two spacious floors in a major office building on New York's Upper West Side.

Current clients include Robert De Niro, Madonna, and Lou Piniella. In the past, Padell's firm has represented such celebrities as Montgomery Clift, Elizabeth Taylor, and Joe DiMaggio.

Padell's personal collection of show business memorabilia rivals the assemblage of baseball collectibles that adorn his office walls.

He has personalized portraits of many stars, and his collection features copies of gold and platinum records awarded to the musical stars he represents.

From his childhood Padell has had a fascination with baseball and its players. "I wanted to get autographs from as many big leaguers as possible, and by going through issues of *The Sporting News*, I was able to get the addresses of many players. Stamps at that time cost 3¢ apiece, and in those days I had very little money to toss around. I was just a kid with limited means at the time, and the autographs I got through the mail meant a lot to me. They gave me a sense of owning something valuable. And I gained those times of value through sheer perseverance."

In January 1948, at the age of 14, Padell sent letters to the New York Giants, New York Yankees, and Brooklyn Dodgers offering his services to become their batboy. He was initially rejected by each team. Finally, however, Eddie Logan, the Giants' clubhouse manager, was so impressed with the boy's intensity and love for baseball that he told the young Padell, "Tell you what, kid, you got the job as assistant visiting batboy. I'm making this position available just for you. I'll pay you $2 a game."

Padell remembers, "I walked away with tears in my eyes. I just couldn't believe that this young kid from the Bronx could become assistant visiting batboy for the famous New York Giants. On my first day of work, I met such guys as BoBo Newsom, Jack Lohrke, and Whitey Lockman. I became pals with the Giants players, and I started to catch batting practice while wearing street clothes. Mel Ott was the Giants manager at the time, and when he was fired early in the season, Leo Durocher succeeded him. When Leo spotted me catching batting practice, he told the clubhouse manager to give me a uniform. One day, the regular visiting batboy got killed in a hunting accident, and I took over his position."

Then in about mid-August, the Yankees, who had heard of Padell, asked if he could serve as their batboy for a couple of weeks while their regular batboy had to serve in an army reserve unit. Since the Giants were on the road, Padell jumped at the chance.

He says, "After the season ended, the Yankees told me they would like to make me their regular batboy for the 1949 season. I told them I couldn't do it unless I spoke to Eddie Logan first. Eddie without hesitation said it would be okay with him and was appreciative of the fact that I did ask permission. He wished me good luck. Shortly after that point, a headline appeared in the sports section of the *New York Sun* reading, 'Giants Trade Batboy to the Yankees.' They were writing about me!"

Padell spent the entire 1949 and 1950 season with the Yankees as their batboy. In the 1949 season, he recalls, "I established a close relationship with Joe DiMaggio, who was bothered by a serious Achilles' heel problem for the first half of that season. I would train with him, catching flies alongside him in the outfield, pitching batting practice to him."

He recalls one game in particular from that 1949 campaign. "It was late in September and the Yankees were playing the Boston Red Sox in a crucial game that went a long way in deciding the pennant. I was positioned near the batter's circle, ready to hand a bat to a Yankee, but the umpire looked over at me and threw me out of the game for supposedly stealing signals from the Red Sox pitcher and two Boston coaches. It was the Red Sox manager Joe McCarthy, a wise old owl, who first caught me in the act. Yankees manager Casey Stengel came over, laid a hand on my shoulder and said gently, 'That's all for you today, kid. Go take a shower.' As far as I know, I was the first batboy ever to be tossed out of a game."

Padell recalls those moments, which occurred in a game a half-century ago, with great fondness. "That's how close I was with the Yankees. I wanted to do everything in my power to help them in any way, and, in that game, I guess I got carried away, because I overstepped my bounds."

The Yankees went on to win the pennant by the razor-thin margin of one game over Boston, and then beat the Brooklyn Dodgers in the World Series 4 games to 1.

Padell concludes, "Those were just about the best days of my life. DiMaggio came back all the way in the last half of '49 as he averaged a lofty .346 and drove in 67 runs. The Yankees also took the pennant in 1950, this time by a three-game margin over the Detroit Tigers, and in the World Series, we beat the Philadelphia Phillies in four straight. Working two straight World Series as a batboy was the thrill of a lifetime.

"Today I run a company that employs about a hundred people, a company that has international reach, but nothing can beat those days when I was a teenager, making two bucks a game as batboy for the World Champion New York Yankees."

Q&A

Temporary Ejections

Back in the early 1950s National League umpires had trouble with Brooklyn Dodgers "bench jockeys" who repeatedly questioned home-plate umpire ball-and-strike calls. Several times the plate umpire ejected all of the Dodgers on the bench who were not in the regular lineup that day.

In a case like this one, would the players be banished for the entire game?

Answer: Rule 4.08 PENALTY—In such a situation the umpire may clear the bench, but he must permit the dismissed players to return to the playing field for substitution, if needed.

Bill Sharman, the extraordinary basketball player, coach, and front-office executive, was one of those Dodgers players who was dismissed in a mass exit. Today he is also a footnote to the trivia of baseball history: he has been the only person who never played in a major-league baseball game who was thrown out of one.

Who Can Sit on the Bench?

Two questions. One, can a player who is on the disabled list sit on his team's bench during an official game; and two, can such a player, once he is granted permission, be requested to leave the bench during a game?

Answer: The answer to both questions is "yes," but in the first case the opposing manager, has to give the permission and in the second case, has to make the request.

This bizarre combination of compliances occurred some years ago in the National League. Frank Lucchesi, manager of the Phillies at the time, made the request of Gene Mauch, skipper of the Expos. Lucchesi wanted Dick Selma, an injured Phillies pitcher, to stay on his bench. Mauch gave his consent.

But Selma didn't like Mauch, so he loudly criticized Gene's every move during the game. In the sixth inning Mauch had had enough. He came out of his dugout and said to the umpire, "Selma has to go. I can't take him anymore."

Exit Selma. Rule 3.06.

Whose Call?

An hour before a game between the Padres and the Cubs, heavy rain descends upon Wrigley Field in Chicago and saturates the playing field. Shortly before the game, as the respective managers bring their lineups to home plate, Cub skipper Don Zimmer informs the umpires that he is canceling the game.

Does he have that right? Suppose the game had already started when the heavy rain fell. Who would then have the authority to halt play permanently?

Answer: The home-team manager, with two exceptions, has the authority to postpone the game before it starts. First, if the initial game of a doubleheader has been played, the umpire-in-chief of the first game decides if the second game should start. Second, in the last series of the season between any two clubs, the league president can exercise the authority, which he usually does by authorizing an umpire to make the decision for him. Once the home-plate umpire receives the lineups from the respective managers, the decision to start or postpone a game lies solely with the umpire-in-chief. Rule 3.10 a–b.

Standard Procedure

Here's one to test your understanding of what managers always do in a volatile situation. To set the stage, let's say it's the bottom of the ninth in a tie game. With one out, the home team has a runner on third. As the manager of the team in the field, how should you align your outfielders? (The question refers to the depth of the outfielders.)

Answer: Just as a manager will have his infield play in when he wants them to cut down a run at the plate in certain circumstances, in our scenario the outfield, too, must be shallow. Each outfielder knows how strong or weak his arm is and will play accordingly. A man like Larry Walker could be a bit deeper than a Juan Gonzalez.

No matter how strong the hitter, the outfield won't be very deep. After all, what good is it to catch a deep blast off the bat of an opposing slugger for out number two if the runner on third is going to tag to win the game? So, you must play at a depth where you have a chance to gun down the runner. Another consideration is that an outfielder who has come in some will be able to catch a sinking line drive that would've fallen in otherwise. No run will score on such a play, and you'll record a big out.

Quotations

In discussing his team's home park: "When you come to the plate in this ballpark, you're in scoring position"?

—*Don Baylor*

"Stay close in the early innings, and I'll think of something"?

—*Charlie Dressen*

"I think there should be bad blood between all teams"?

—*Earl Weaver*

Saddled with an inept team, Casey Stengel moaned, "Can't anyone here play this game?"

"You don't save a pitcher for tomorrow. Tomor-row it may rain"? He's also famous for saying, "Nice guys finish last"—although that wasn't exactly what he said.

—*Leo Durocher*

After suffering through a tough road trip, Ray Knight said, "When it rains it pours, and we're in the midst of a monsoon"?

Even though he'd won a World Series in the 1990s, this manager once muttered, "I'm not sure whether I'd rather be managing or testing bulletproof vests."

—*Joe Torre*

This man's team was plagued by injuries in 1989, prompting him to observe, "If World War III broke out, I'd guarantee you we'd win the pennant by 20 games. All our guys would be 4-F. They couldn't pass the physical."

—*Whitey Herzog*

In 1997, this White Sox skipper philosophized, "I learned a long time ago, in this game you might as well take the blame because you're going to get it anyway."
— *Terry Bevington*

His pitcher entered the game with the bases loaded. Two wild pitches later, the bases were empty because all three men had scored, leading to this managerial quip: "Well, that's one way to pitch out of a bases-loaded jam." Clue: He was managing the Brewers when this occurred.
— *Tom Trebelhorn*

Lucky enough to be the manager of George Brett, this man was asked what he told Brett regarding hitting. The manager replied, "I tell him, 'Attaway to hit, George.'"
— *Jim Frey*

Never known for his use of grammar, this great manager once said of a player's injury: "There's nothing wrong with his shoulder except some pain, and pain don't hurt you."
— *Sparky Anderson*

On what it takes to be a successful manager, an all-time big-name manager opined, "A sense of humor and a good bullpen."
— *Whitey Herzog*

Two quotes from the same man. A) "I'm not the manager because I'm always right, but I'm always right because I'm the manager." B) "The worst thing about managing is the day you realize you want to win more than your players do."
— *Gene Mauch*

This manager for one day naively believed, "Managing isn't all that difficult. Just score more runs than the other guy."

—*Ted Turner*

This manager summarized the future of two 20-year-old prospects, saying, "In ten years, Ed Kranepool has a chance to be a star. In ten years, Greg Goosen has a chance to be thirty."

—*Casey Stengal*

Who said: "We live by the Golden Rule—those who have the gold make the rules."?

—*Buzzi Bavasi*

This manager did so well, that owner August Busch, who was 85 at the time, told him he could have a lifetime contract. The St. Louis skipper countered with, "Whose lifetime? Yours or mine?"

—*Whitey Herzog*

This peppery manager would upstage umpires at the drop of a hat. He even looked to peck umps with the beak of his hat. He offered one of his most famous lines after he showed up the umpires by taking a rule book out on the field. He stated, "There ain't no rule in the rule book about bringing a rule book on the field."

—*Earl Weaver*

CHAPTER

Off the Field

A Mickey Mantle Tale

Longtime Detroit Tiger announcer Ernie Harwell recalled what had to be one of the longest singles in the history of the game. He said, "I saw Mickey Mantle hit a ball that bounced into the center-field bleachers at Yankee Stadium. He hit it with the bases loaded in an extra-inning game.

"At first, they gave him a ground-rule double, then they looked it up and could only award him a single." According to the rule book, the batter is awarded a single since it only took a single to drive in the run from third. The only exception to this rule is a game-winning home run. In that situation, they do not take away the homer even if a lesser hit would have won the game (as was the case with Mantle).

Joe Pepitone Orders 2000 Hamburgers in One Fell Swoop at a Chicago White Castle

Joe Pepitone, at 57, still looked every inch the athlete and he always dressed to the nines: tailored charcoal suit, tailored shirt, fancy ties, Italian custom-made shoes, and a bit of jewelry.

We presumptuously asked, "Joe, what did that suit cost you, 2,500 bucks?" Pepi answered, "Not exactly, but you're not too far off."

We then asked Pepitone of his remembrances of his experiences in the Japanese professional leagues. Pepi said, "I really wasn't too happy in Japan because I felt like I was an alien there. But I've followed the game over the years and am impressed with the fact that so many Japanese guys are now playing in the American major leagues, and several of them have become stars. The Japanese are really serious about baseball. They like to imitate American styles, and there are so many American-based companies selling their stuff in Japan, like Pepsi, Coke, McDonald's and others."

"Were the McDonald's hamburgers really going for $5 a crack when you were in Japan, as you wrote in your *New York Times* article?"

Pepitone replied, "I might have exaggerated a bit on that point, but living in Japan is expensive. You've got to remember that they have to import a lot of things necessary to keep them going."

At this point, Pepitone became quite talkative and recalled another story dealing with hamburgers and baseball. He told us, "Back in 1971, when I was with the Chicago Cubs, I really had a good year and batted over .300 for the first and only time in my career. I got along well with our manager, Leo Durocher, and became something of a celebrity in Chicago. Remember, I was basically a

Brooklyn/New York guy. I was invited to lots of TV and radio shows, and one day one of the interviewers asked me what I liked best about Chicago. I said that I liked the hamburgers at the White Castles in and around the Chicago Loop. I went on and on, saying that White Castle served really terrific hamburgers.

"A few day later, I received a package from White Castle headquarters in Chicago. What did the package contain? There was a bundle of 2,000 coupons, each one good for a free hamburger. How the hell could I eat 2,000 hamburgers? But a couple of weeks after I received that bag full of coupons, I went down to a White Castle in the heart of Chicago's Loop district threw down all 2,000 coupons on the counter and demanded 2,000 hamburgers. The manager was astounded and asked me how I could possibly eat 2,000 hamburgers. I said, 'Just bring out those 2,000 burgers and we'll hold an open house for anyone who wants one for free.'

"Then I screamed, 'Burgers on the house, compliments of Joe Pepitone!' Within a few minutes the place was jammed. White Castle didn't have enough counter guys on duty to handle the traffic, and so they let me put on a chef's hat and apron, and I dished out hundreds of burgers. This White Castle began running out of burgers before we hit the one thousand mark, and so they had to bring in additional stuff from other White Castles in the Chicago metro area. Finally, after several hours, White Castle honored all those 2,000 coupons, and everyone went home happy."

Pepitone concluded by saying, "White Castle in Chicago was really happy about this big hamburger giveaway, since this story got into all of the big Chicago newspapers and was published on all the major radio and TV stations."

As the old saying goes in press agencies, "I don't care what you say about me, but just mention my name."

For Bouton, Let Bygones Be Bygones

Officials at the New York Public Library listed Jim Bouton's *Ball Four* as "one of the most influential of a list of 100 books published in the United States during the 20th century." That list included books published on all subjects—not just on sports and baseball. Bouton recounted his baseball career's trials and tribulations. He was also critical of his New York Yankees teammates, including Mickey Mantle, one of the all-time great Yankee heroes. Many members of the Yankees never forgave Bouton for portraying Mickey in a bad light, and they swore never to speak to him again.

Because of *Ball Four* and its repercussions, Bouton was never invited to any of the Yankees Old-Timers' Days staged annually at around mid-season—that is, until the 1998 Old-Timers' Day staged in late July of that year. George Steinbrenner, principal owner of the Yankees, had continuously enforced the "ban" on Bouton from Old-Timers' Day, although he bought the Yankees in 1973—five years after the controversial author left the Bronx Bombers.

The ice was finally broken after Michael Bouton, the ex-pitcher's son, wrote an impassioned article in the June 21, 1998, issue of the Sunday *New York Times*. The article was titled "For Bouton, Let Bygones Be Bygones," and subtitled "Son's Wish on Father's Day Is to See Dad and Yogi Stand With Old-Timers."

As soon as George Steinbrenner read the article he called the elder Bouton and invited him to attend. Jim Bouton appeared at his first Yankees Old-Timers' Day ever and for the first time in 30 years wore the pinstripes of the Bronx Bombers. Bouton said, "Wearing that Yankee uniform again brought all those happy memories back when I was a kid in his 20's pitching for the best team in baseball history. I felt like I've finally been admitted back into the family. And my son, Michael, really knows how to write."

Hall of Famers' Salaries Before the Age of Television

Back in the so-called "good old days," most big league baseball players, even the biggest stars, hustled around to find temporary jobs in the off-season. During the 1940s and 1950s, many of the game's biggest stars—the Hall of Famers—held everyday jobs. Duke Snider, Brooklyn Dodgers outfielder, carried mail from the Brooklyn post office during the holiday period; Stan Musial, St. Louis Cardinals outfielder/first baseman, worked as a clerk in his father-in-law's grocery store in Donora, Pennsylvania; Phil Rizzuto, New York Yankees shortstop, worked as a salesman in a New York men's clothing store; Mike Garcia, of the Cleveland Indians, worked in a Cleveland dry cleaning shop and then bought the business; Bob Feller, also of the Cleveland Indians sold insurance and then opened his own insurance company (which eventually went bankrupt); Early Wynn of the Washington Senators, Chicago White Sox, and Cleveland Indians was a construction laborer and then head of his own construction company in Alabama; and Carl Furillo of the Brooklyn Dodgers, was an elevator repairman in Manhattan. We could list countless other stars who had to take on ordinary jobs following their playing careers, and those who had to work at odd jobs in the off-season in order to provide for their families.

It's been only within the past generation or so that baseball salaries have skyrocketed. Nowadays a player who signs a big multi-year contract is usually financially set for life.

We can state the reason for the almost geometric increase in baseball salaries in a single word: television. Back when baseball games were first televised in the late 1940s and early 1950s, there were many baseball experts who maintained that TV would "kill" attendance at games. These so-called "experts" said, "Why would anyone go to a game if he could see it for free on TV?" It so happened that TV got many millions of new fans interested in the game, with box office receipts zooming as a result.

Back during the 1920s and 1930s when ballgames were broadcast on radio, revenues from that source were almost inconsequential. In many cases, major league teams waived potential broadcast fees because they were happy just to get the free publicity.

The Cleveland Indians received their first "big" TV contract from station WXEL in 1951. That contract called for WXEL to broadcast all of the Indians' 77 home games, plus six games on the road. For those 83 games, the Indians received $250,000—a lot of money in those days; in fact, enough money to cover more than half the players' salaries.

Minimum salaries were not agreed upon until the late 1940s. When Jackie Robinson, the first black player in the major leagues, was promoted from the Montreal Royals of the International League in 1947 to the Brooklyn Dodgers under general manager Branch Rickey, he was given a $5,000 contract—the big league minimum at the time. Player salaries before that time were generally paltry.

Then there's Jeff Heath, a Cleveland Indians outfielder from 1936 to 1945. He continuously complained about having to play for "peanuts." After he hit .343 and drove in 112 runs for Cleveland in 1938, he was given a contract for the 1939 campaign for about $3,000—the equivalent of a Cleveland public school teacher's salary at the time.

After Heath finished his big league career with the Boston Braves in 1949, he signed a contract with the Pacific Coast League's Seattle Rainiers in 1950 worth $25,000—the highest salary by far he had ever received in baseball. In fact, no minor league player up to that point was given that type of generous contract.

Baseball salaries during the Depression era of the 1930s

were generally very low, even for the biggest stars. Frank "Lefty" O'Doul led the National League in batting in 1932 while with the Brooklyn Dodgers. He averaged a fat .368. Did he get a raise for that performance? No. He was cut $1,000, down from $8,000 to $7,000, but he still ranked among the top-paid big leaguers.

In 1940, Lou Boudreau, star shortstop of the Cleveland Indians, played in every one of the team's 155 games, averaging a solid .295, driving in 101 runs, and leading American League shortstops with a .986 fielding percentage. For that grand effort Boudreau played under a contract calling for the munificent sum of $5,000—which amounted to little more than $30 per game.

Indians' owner Alva Bradley, a business tycoon with interests in myriad industries, felt guilty about that contract, so he gave Boudreau a $2,000 bonus at season's close. Then Bradley doubled Boudreau's salary to $10,000—making him one of the higher-paid players in the big leagues.

The New York Yankees— Tight With a Buck

The New York Yankees, baseball's most successful franchise, had the reputation of being extremely "tight with a buck"—at least until George Steinbrenner bought the team in 1973.

Take the tale of Babe Ruth, whose relations with the Yankees were strained after he retired from active play in 1935. At the beginning of the 1939 season, he wrote to the Yankees' offices and requested a pair of complimentary tickets for opening day at Yankee Stadium. Ruth was curtly told by return mail that he must include his check with his request. Naturally, Ruth, who felt grievously insulted, was not present for opening day ceremonies.

Then we have the case of Phil Rizzuto. When he was doing play-by-play for the Yankees on radio and TV, he often recalled the time he hit his first homer for New York at Yankee Stadium early in 1941, his rookie season. As Rizzuto rounded third base, a fan ran onto the field, grabbed Phil's cap off the top of his head, and disappeared into the stands with it.

The next day Rizzuto received a note form George Weiss, the Yankees general manager, saying that $5 would be deducted from his pay for losing the cap. Rizzuto said, "I couldn't help it. That fan came after me like a madman."

Weiss said firmly, "You've got to hold onto your stuff better." The $5 charge stood.

Babe Ruth Still a Major Force in Advertising

Babe Ruth still remains a force in advertising, though he passed to the "Great Beyond" more than a half-century ago. Any individual or commercial enterprise must pay his estate a royalty for using his name or image. For more than a decade, the Ruth name and image have been represented by Curtis Management, Inc., in Indianapolis, Indiana. Ruth's estate has received more than $1 million dollars a year in royalties in recent years. The Babe is survived by a number of children and grandchildren, as well as by other heirs, who share in the royalties.

Ruth was even "resurrected" recently in a series of food product radio commercials with Phil Rizzuto, former New York Yankees shortstop and a member of baseball's Hall of Fame. Ruth's voice was of course simulated by an actor in these commercials.

The Babe Ruth Union Suit, a Best Seller

During his long, dramatic, and tumultuous big-league baseball career, George Herman "Babe" Ruth, the Sultan of Swat, endorsed scores of commercial products, such as cigars, chewing tobacco, cigarettes, beer, meat products, various types of bread, automobiles, shirts, hats, golf clubs, baseball bats, and gloves. He also endorsed restaurants and other types of business establishments, especially those located in New York City.

Most of Ruth's advertising contracts were handled by Christy Walsh, baseball's first major agent. Walsh, an attorney and noted journalist, did not negotiate player contracts, but he became an expert in structuring endorsement contacts.

One of the most lucrative deals Walsh struck for Ruth was with McLoughlin Manufacturing Company of Kokomo, Indiana. This association began in 1926—a time when the Babe was at the absolute peak of his career.

McLoughlin Manufacturing was one of the country's leading producers of men's underwear, or "union suits," as they were called then. The relationship continued without interruption until Ruth's death on August 16, 1948.

The Babe Ruth portrait and facsimile signature came on all packages containing the union suits. As a result, sales zoomed.

McLoughlin Manufacturing was headquartered in a sprawling redbrick building in Kokomo, a town of some 50,000 population in the north-central part of the Hoosier state. On top of the building stood a bulbous water tower marked with an inscription reading "McLoughlin Manufacturing Company, Home of Babe Ruth Union Suits."

Crazy, but true!

Ruth was paid a royalty on every McLoughlin Union Suit endorsed by him with his photo and facsimile signature on every box. During the course of more than two decades, he earned tens of thousands of dollars in royalty payments. The endorsement contracts between Ruth and McLoughlin were renewed annually.

Barry Halper, the baseball memorabilia collector based in northern New Jersey, and part-owner of the New York Yankees, has a ring binder containing all the documents relating to the Ruth–McLoughlin deal. The documents bear the Ruth signature, together with those of Christy Walsh and McLoughlin executives. That esoteric assemblage of Ruth memorabilia today is worth a small fortune.

Babe Ruth's reputation as an American icon has grown to such great heights over the years that a near-mint package of his McLoughlin Manufacturing Company union suits is worth thousands of dollars on the current sports memorabilia marketplace.

Henry Aaron—Autographs, Yes; Registration Signatures, No.

When anyone registers at a hotel or motel just about any-place in the world, he must sign the registration book. But not Henry Aaron, the great home-run slugger.

When Aaron appeared as an autograph guest at a show featuring all living major leaguers who had rapped out at least 3,000 base hits,—an event staged at Atlantic City's Showboat Hotel and Casino in the fall of 1995—he flat out refused to sign the registry. "No way I'm going to sign that book!" Henry told the hotel clerk.

It seemed that Aaron's fee per autograph at the Showboat ranged from about $50 to more than $100, depending upon the nature of the item to be signed. (Autographed bats are the most expensive.) Henry Aaron simply wasn't going to sign anything for free.

The matter was settled when Aaron's agent signed the registry for him.

DiMaggio Retains His Title as 'The Human Signing Machine'

Joe DiMaggio, the great New York Yankees center fielder who sparkled on the diamonds for 13 seasons between 1936 and 1951 (with three years out for service during World War II), was named "The Greatest Living Ex-Ballplayer" at a 1969 conclave staged at the White House and hosted by President Richard M. Nixon. The event marked the centenary of professional baseball in the United States.

For the first several years of his career, DiMaggio felt he was badly underpaid by the Yankees. After having three sensational seasons, starting with his rookie year in 1936, "Joltin' Joe" held out for about three weeks at the start of the 1939 season in order to land a contract for $30,000—a lot of money in those days, but peanuts compared with today's boxcar salaries for star ballplayers.

By the time DiMaggio retired after the 1951 season, his salary had reached the $100,000 plateau—top money in those days, but less than each player, manager, and coach receives today through licensing agreements arranged through the Major League Players Association. (Licensing money comes from royalties for commercial use of the Major League Baseball and individual team logos. The value of the dollar has, of course, changed radically over the past half-century.)

However, whatever amount DiMaggio earned in salary in his 13-year big league career—a total that may add up to a tad over $1 million, including checks from playing in ten World Series—it pales in significance to the money he subsequently piled up as a result of his singular place in the history of the game.

Over the many years since he retired from active play, DiMaggio signed so many autographs for various fees that he became known as "The Human Signing Machine."

DiMag commanded the highest rate per autograph in the late 1980s—$15. Joltin' Joe was being criticized in the press for being the "Yankee Clipper," but he did not bow to derision. In response to the criticism, DiMag simply raised his rate to $18. Whenever he appeared at a "card show," fans flocked to his signing table in droves.

Through the 1990s, the DiMaggio rate for an autograph rose steadily, so that by 1999, he would command $150 to autograph a baseball, $175 for a photograph, and $350 for a Yankees cap! Thus, he had developed a "scale," according to the type of item. Autographed game-used caps brought even bigger bucks, as we'll see.

Throughout the 1980s and into the late 1990s, DiMaggio appeared at card shows staged at a variety of venues: at hotels in midtown Manhattan; at the Meadowlands Hilton in Secaucus, New Jersey; at Hofstra University in Hempstead, Long Island; in Chicago; and at the big casino hotels in Atlantic City. In addition to his autographing fees, the show promoters also had to pay for all his travel expenses. Joe was a very sharp businessman and he knew the hold he had on baseball fans and memorabilia collectors.

Strangely enough, DiMaggio refused to sign a wide array of baseball memorabilia items for reasons only known by him. For example, at an early 1990s card show held at the Meadowlands Hilton, there was a sign at the hotel's exhibition center entrance reading:

Mr. DiMaggio will not sign the following types of items:
• Baseballs already signed by anyone else
• Original artwork portraying Mr. DiMaggio
• Baseball bats
• Baseball jerseys

On another occasion in the early 1990s, a baseball memorabilia collector traveled several hundred miles to the Meadowlands Hilton in order to have DiMaggio sign an original artwork showing him in a classic batting pose. DiMag flatly refused. The collector said in disgust, "I get on the road for hours just to have the painting signed, and DiMaggio just said, 'No.'"

DiMaggio knew that the value of the painting would multiply by some three to four times with his signature, and he didn't want anyone to make an undue profit. (Pete Rose, the all-time major league base-hit king, on the other hand, will sign anything thrust down on his autograph table. We've even seen Rose sign copies of *The Dowd Report*, a volume published by the Baseball Commissioner's Office that dealt with Rose's alleged Baseball gambling. Rose, some fans say, is as an "equal opportunity signer.")

DiMaggio's Big Bucks for Signing Baseball Bats

While Joseph Paul DiMaggio refused to sign baseball bats at card shows, he did autograph lumber under special circumstances—and if the price was right. And DiMag's rates for bat signings were not cheap. There's something special about having a big star of the game sign a bat, especially one in the rare upper echelons of the Hall of Fame like Joe DiMaggio.

Of all of his deeds on the diamond, DiMaggio is perhaps best known for his 56-game hitting streak in 1941. Most baseball historians feel that this is one of the records that will not be broken. (Standing in second place for a consecutive hitting streak is Pete Rose, who batted safely in 44 straight games while with Cincinnati in 1978—that's the National League record.)

DiMaggio signed bats for free for fans earlier in his playing days, but he stopped that altogether when the autograph craze started taking off in the early 1980s. Sometime toward the end of 1990, an ambitious promoter asked DiMaggio if he would sign 1,941 bats to commemorate the 50th anniversary of his 1,941 hitting streak. The promoter made DiMaggio an offer he could not refuse. He would pay the old Yankee Clipper exactly $2,000 for each signed bat. The promoter then proceeded to advertise the bats at $3,995 each!

DiMaggio, working in a private office, spent nearly three full days signing those 1,941 bats. For those labors, his check came out to a little under $3.9 million. No sports person in the history of this planet has made more than $3.9 million for less than three days' work.

For a weekend card show, DiMaggio often cleared more than $100,000. In some cases, the promoter would take not a penny from that amount. He'd use DiMaggio as a "loss leader." The number of fans jamming into the place because of Joltin' Joe's presence would attract more business.

In the few years before his death, Joe was bringing in his own attorney to monitor these shows because he didn't want to miscount the number of autographs he signed. Remember, there was big money involved. Whenever there was a Joe D signing session, there was a big-business atmosphere that reeked of the "Fortune 500."

DiMaggio was also a stickler for "expenses" incurred while starring as an autograph guest at card shows. In a late 1990s card show appearance, he tacked on a $6.00 charge for taxi fare. We've got to watch those nickels!

Please don't misunderstand us, we fully appreciate Joe DiMaggio's contribution to the game of baseball and to American folklore. We interviewed this baseball great on numerous occasions and he was always a gentleman. In fact, we consider ourselves lucky because Joe didn't ordinarily grant interviews to reporters. And he was always more than happy to give us a free autograph, which we gave out to friends. Thus, we established a personal relationship with him and stand in awe at his accomplishments.

DiMaggio's strange hold upon the American sporting public was dramatically illustrated at a mid-1990s card show appearance he made at Hofstra University. The show was staged at Hofstra's cavernous Fitness Center on an early Saturday afternoon, with over 1,000 people present, plus some 75 dealers, and several ex-star players as autograph guests. As Joe entered the room, a sudden hush fell over the crowd as all eyes strained to get a glimpse of the former Yankee great, then past 80 with a shock of pure white hair. DiMaggio, slightly stooped and with a history of medical problems, still maintained the majestic stride of a superathlete. Fathers lifted their small sons onto their shoulders so they could get a look at a true baseball icon, a legend in every sense of the word. This scene was of such magnitude that it could never be forgotten.

DiMaggio always took his appearances as an autograph guest very seriously. He dressed impeccably—a tailored suit, tailored shirt, and silk tie. And even as he passed his 80th birthday, his signature remained clear and bold. He always took his time and signed carefully. Many big-time athletes just scrawl their signature at card shows.

At earlier card shows, DiMaggio would personalize any autograph, but starting in the early 1990s, he would sign his name only. At a full-fledged card show, he'd do 1,000 autographs on a Saturday, and then another 1,000 on Sunday; he just couldn't take the time to write out personalizations.

DiMaggio Uniform Parts Set Record at Auction

Anything connected with Joe DiMaggio creates serious interest and big money. For example, a public auction staged in New Jersey in March 1998 featured various pieces of equipment Joltin' Joe used during his career with the Yankees.

A pair of size 11 black spikes DiMag wore during the 1941 season was purchased for $36,094 (including the 15% buyer's premiums). The spikes took on greater value because they were autographed by DiMaggio. That figure stands as a record realization for any example of game-worn baseball spikes.

At the same auction, an autographed game-worn Yankees home pinstripe jersey worn by DiMaggio during the 1947 season realized $82,027.

Other DiMaggio items that brought hefty prices at this New Jersey auction included:
- a 1942 autographed game-used cap for $22,188;
- a circa 1950 game-used bat (not autographed) for $8,630;
- a pair of autographed game-used pants (circa 1950) for $6,606; and
- a 1941 Yankee Stadium ticket from DiMaggio's 44th-hit streak game for $649.

Perhaps the most unusual of all DiMaggio memorabilia specimens was offered by Sotheby's on February 29, 1992, at its sprawling New York City galleries. The item was a piece of wedding cake from DiMaggio's marriage on November 19, 1939, to actress Dorothy Arnold in San Francisco. It found a buyer at $1,210, against a "modest" $500/600 estimate. The more than half-century-old hunk of wedding cake, hard as a rock and wrapped in cellophane, came with two bisque columns and a rose decoration from the cake, together with the invitation to the wedding and reception, and a photo of Joe and Mrs. DiMaggio cutting the cake!

This particular lot went to a specialist in Joe DiMaggio memorabilia who said he'd be happy to pay top dollar for anything connected with the old Yankee Clipper.

After battling a series of illnesses for several months, Joe DiMaggio died on March 8, 1999, at the age of 84 at his Florida home. As long as baseball is played, Joe DiMaggio's name will be remembered. He left us not only with an array of records and deeds achieved on the diamond, but he also left sports hobbyists with literally hundreds of thousands of baseball collectibles he had personally signed. Who knows—that figure may be well over a million.

Mark McGwire's 70th Home Run Ball Sells for $3,005,000 at Auction

The baseball hammered out by Mark McGwire on September 27, 1998, at Busch Stadium in St. Louis for his record-breaking 70th home run, brought an incredible $3,005,000 at a public auction staged at New York City's Madison Square Garden on January 12, 1999. The hammer price came to $2,700,000. With the auction house's commission, the total realization added up to $3,005,000.

It goes almost without saying that this marks the highest realization for any single item of baseball memorabilia sold at public auction. The winning bid was cast by Todd McFarlane, 37, a native of Calgary, Alberta, and now a resident of Tempe, Arizona. McFarlane, who claimed he spent his life's savings on this historic baseball, heads his own company, Todd McFarlane Productions, which produces a wide variety of comic books and related products. McFarlane, who is also a part-owner of the Edmonton Oilers in the National Hockey League, calls himself a "psycho baseball fan."

New official major league baseballs, produced in a factory in Costa Rica, retail for less than $5.

It's Alexander Cartwright, Not Abner Doubleday, Who Invented Baseball!

John Sterling and Michael Kay were partners on radio broadcasts of Yankees games for over a decade. Although we over appreciate their general knowledge of the game and its wide array of intricacies, they have their zany moments on the radio.

Michael Kay once went into a soliloquy on the beauty and symmetry of the game during a Yankees broadcast early in the 1998 season. Toward the midpoint of the game, a player hit a grounder to deep short, with the shortstop coming up with the ball and throwing in time to the first baseman to get the out. Kay in effect said, "That's beautiful... in the great majority of the cases, if an infielder handles the ball cleanly, his throw to first will get the batter out. The space between the bases, 90 feet apart, is just perfect. Thank you, General Doubleday, for inventing this great game."

The only problem with Kay's analysis is that General Abner Doubleday did not invent the game at Cooperstown, New York, in 1839, where the first ballgame was supposed to have been played. It has been proven that Doubleday (1819–1893) never set foot in Cooperstown and had nothing to do with the development of baseball. Even historians at the Hall of Fame in Cooperstown agree, although Doubleday's mistaken connection with the diamond game is legendary.

Credit for the development of modern baseball, as we know the game, must go to Alexander Joy Cartwright (1820–1892), who organized the first baseball team, the Knickerbocker Ball Club of New York City, in 1845. Cartwright's Knickerbockers played the first organized game on June 19, 1846, at the Elysian Fields, Hoboken, New Jersey, against a club called the New Yorks.

It was Cartwright, an engineer and New York City volunteer fireman, who set the basic rules of the game that stand today, including ending the early practice of putting a man out by hitting him with a thrown ball. He introduced the nine-man team with an unalterable batting order; the nine-inning game, three outs per side; and the 90-foot baseline. He also dressed up his team, composed of local firefighters, in the game's first uniforms. Most New York teams of that era came out of firehouses. Barry Halper, the indefatigable New Jersey memorabilia collector, has a wide array of Cartwright materials, including his fireman's hat and fireman's horn!

For his contributions to baseball, Alexander Cartwright was inducted into the Hall of Fame in 1938. Though there is a Doubleday exhibit in the Hall of Fame, Abner Doubleday was never elected into baseball's shrine.

The next time Michael Kay muses about the wonder of the 90-foot baselines, he should say instead, "Thank you, Mr. Cartwright."

Catching Baseballs
Thrown Off of Tall Buildings

Charles "Gabby" Street, who gained fame first as Walter Johnson's "personal catcher" with the Washington Senators and later as a pennant-winning manager of the St. Louis Cardinals in 1930–1931, was destined to be best remembered for an offbeat stunt performed in the nation's capital on the morning of August 21, 1908.

Prompted by a bet between two local sportsmen, Street won a $500 prize and worldwide publicity by catching a baseball thrown by Johnson from the top of the 555-foot high Washington Monument. Though considerably jarred by the impact of the ball as it landed in his glove, Street was still able to be the catcher at Walter Johnson's 3–1 victory over the Detroit Tigers that afternoon. It was said that Street's experience on the receiving end of Johnson's "cannonballs" had uniquely prepared him to accomplish the feat at the Washington Monument feat.

Several years later, Brooklyn Dodgers manager and former catcher Wilbert Robinson was supposed to catch a baseball thrown from the top of a newly-built New York City skyscraper. Prankster Casey Stengel, a young Brooklyn outfielder, substituted a large grapefruit for the baseball. Robinson made the catch but was furious when he found himself covered with grapefruit pulp.

In mid-season 1938, Cleveland Indians back-up catcher Hank Helf caught a ball thrown from near the top of the 708-foot Terminal Tower (then America's tallest skyscraper outside New York City). Helf made the catch, and today his name is still remembered for that performance.

Baseballs dropped from the height of skyscrapers travel more than 150 miles an hour when they reach the ground. Stunt catches of such balls have, for all intents and purposes, been banned as too dangerous by major league baseball.

'Splashy' New Ballpark Innovations

The Arizona Diamondbacks, based in Phoenix, became the National League's newest franchise in 1998 by going all out in making their new Diamondbacks Stadium one of the most innovative ballparks ever. Chief among the innovations is a swimming pool, together with an adjacent hot tub, beyond the outfield barriers. The pool area is housed in a special section of Diamondbacks Stadium. For season reservations to a half-dozen seats or more, plus access to the pool and its accessories, fans pay more than $4,000 a year. They can also catch some rays on a suntanning deck and, if they want, watch a little baseball.

The Tampa Bay Devil Rays, the American League's newest franchise, which also debuted in 1998, took second place to no one in ballpark innovations when they opened Tropicana Field. At this stadium, fans who get bored with the game can go down to a super-mall underneath the outfield stands and shop for everything from shoes and shirts to new cars.

The San Francisco Giants opened a new ballpark in 2000, also plan a variety of innovations. Chief among these are: a food court, a performance cooking center, and a kid's interactive learning center.

In the *Wall Street Journal*, Sam Walker commented on the new era ballpark phenomena: Critics contend that all the sideshows won't build a true fan base, and once the novelties wear off some operators will lose money. Nevertheless, team owners see it differently; they say the added attractions will lure new groups to the stadiums and prompt them to stay all day and spend a little more.

Quotation

An ex pitcher butchered the English language in his later career as an announcer. In one case, he said a player had "slud into third" instead of "slid." Another of his remarks was, "Don't fail to miss tomorrow's game." The announcer's name? *—Dizzy Dean.*

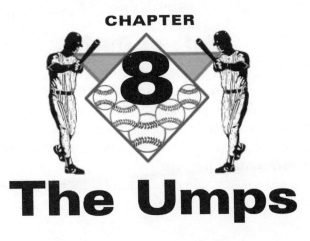

CHAPTER 8

The Umps

Walter's Fastball

When Walter Johnson of the Washington Senators was in his prime, one of his fastballs broke his catcher's hand in the middle innings of a game. Umpire Billy Evans, who was more than a little bit concerned about his own health behind the plate, beseeched the substitute catcher, "For God's sake, protect me, will you?"

Johnson's first pitch to his new catcher bounced off Evans' leg. His next pitch hit Evans on his chest protector. "That's all," Evans wisely proclaimed, tongue in cheek. "Game's called on account of darkness."

Safe or Out?

In a Phillie-Dodger game one evening, umpire Beans Reardon got his messages mixed up. Richie Ashburn came sliding into Brooklyn third baseman Billy Cox, and Reardon shouted safe but signaled out.

"Well, what am I?" Ashburn asked the caught-on-the-horns-of-a-dilemma umpire.

"You heard me say safe," Reardon said. "But 30,000 people saw me signal out. You're outnumbered. Get out of here."

Joker Altrock

Nick Altrock, the third-base coach for the Senators, was an accomplished umpire baiter. One day a couple of calls by umpire Bill McGowan went against Washington, and Altrock explicitly expressed his displeasure with them.

A few innings later a batter fouled a ball into the third-base stands, and McGowan saw a woman being carried out of the park on a stretcher.

"Did the ball hit her?" McGowan asked Altrock.

"No," the coach snidely replied. "You called the last one right, and she fainted."

Stubborn Manager

One day veteran National League umpire Doug Harvey ejected a manager for protesting one of his ball-and-strike calls too passionately. The manager then stood defiantly on home plate and said he wouldn't leave the field. Finally, Harvey told the hitter to get into the batter's box and ordered the pitcher to throw. The hurler hesitated at first, but when he was directed to throw a second time, he hummed a high hard-one close by the manager's head.

"Strike one!" Harvey bellowed.

Before the moundsman's next pitch, the manager had retreated to the safety of his clubhouse.

Sick

Bill Klem, the great umpire, threw Pie Traynor, the great third baseman of the Pirates, out of a game one hot afternoon in Pittsburgh. That surprised both fans and players alike. Traynor was considered to be an umpire's ballplayer.

"What did he say?" the reporters wanted to know after the game.

"He wasn't feeling well," Klem said.

"We didn't know he was ill."

"Well, that's what he said. He told me he was sick of my stupid decisions."

No Use Sliding

One night when Red Schoendienst was managing the Cardinals, he became incensed when umpire Frank Secory called Mike Shannon out on a play at the plate. In trying to prove that Shannon was safe, Schoendienst demonstrated by sliding into home plate himself.

Secory fired his right hand into the air. "Same as Shannon," he said, "you're out, too. Out of the game."

Not Al Kline

Ron Luciano, the former American League umpire, liked to talk to the players. One player he was unsuccessful in talking to was right fielder Al Kaline of the Detroit Tigers.

At the end of a Tiger inning, Kaline would grab his glove and trot out to his position. Luciano, who would be working first base that day, would say, "Hi, Al, how's the family?" Kaline wouldn't respond. Nothing.

That's the way it went for ten years. Then one day, out of the blue, Kaline ran past the umpire and said, "Hi, Ron, how's it going?"

Luciano, who was startled, ran after Kaline, demanding, "Why are you talking to me now? I've been trying to get you to say something for ten years, and you gave me nothing. Why now?"

Kaline replied in a calm and easy voice, "I just wanted to make sure you were going to hang around, Ron."

'Hidden' Ball Play

On July 1, 1998, the Chicago White Sox were playing the Houston Astros when, in a weird variation on the old hid-den ball play, an umpire, not a player, "hid" the ball. Doug Henry was on the mound for Houston, and the Sox had Ray Durham on third.

Atlanta Braves coach Pat Corrales picks up the play-by-play from there: "It looked like the pitch was a sinker, and it hit the ground and bounced up. The ball got by the catcher and went in the umpire's [front] pocket and got buried there.

"The hitter didn't know where it was, the catcher didn't know, and the umpire [Gerry Davis] didn't know. The runner crossed the plate, then everybody realized where the ball was."

Durham scored easily as the befuddled catcher, Brad Ausmus, was the loser in this zany game of hide-and-seek. In reality, according to baseball rules, once a ball is "lost," it is also, in medical terminology, DOA. And once a ball is declared dead, searching for it is pointless. As Corrales pointed out, "If it gets stuck like that, you get one base, once they figured out where the ball was." He called it one of the strangest things he'd ever seen in the majors.

Zany Umpiring in the Japanese Leagues

Umpiring practices in Japan are somewhat different than those in the U.S. professional leagues. For example, in a 1973 game played at Tokyo's sprawling Korakuen Stadium, a player began punching an umpire as the result of a disputed call. Several teammates joined in on the pummeling. Then the team's manager came storming out of the dugout. What did he do? Stop the fight? Heck, no. He also began punching the beleaguered ump!

Unlike American umpires, their Japanese league counterparts change their decisions—sometimes two or three times, depending upon the arguments put forward by the players, coaches, and managers. At a June 1974 game between the Tokyo Giants and the Hanshin Tigers at Korakuen, we witnessed a 45-minute game delay because of umpire indecision. All the while, the Japanese fans remained in their seats, uncomplaining.

In 1974, Joe Lutz, a former major league player and a Cleveland Indians coach, became the first American to manage a team in Japan when he was appointed pilot of the Hiroshima Toya Carp of the Central League. Lutz resigned before the season was over. Why? Because of a controversial call at home plate that went against his team. In that call, the umpire changed his mind three times.

Search and Seizure

The 1987 Yankees had Rickey Henderson on second base and Willie Randolph on first when the White Sox pitcher's sinkerball bounced in front of the plate, caromed off the catcher's equipment, and landed in the home-plate umpire's ball bag.

But no one with the exception of the umpire knew where the ball was. He knew that he had had one ball in his bag. Suddenly he had two. He also had a dilemma. Should he stop the action and award bases? Should he tell the catcher where the ball was and let him search for it? Even if he did, how would he know which ball was the original one? How would you handle his dilemma?

Answer: When this play occurred, there was no rule to cover the situation. But the home-plate umpire appropriately referred to Rule 9.01 c: Each umpire has the authority to rule on any point that is not specifically covered by the rules. The umpire in this instance stopped the action and advanced Henderson to third base and Randolph to second base, which, in his opinion, was where they would have gotten had the ball not landed in his ball bag.

Today, if the ball lodges in the umpire's or the catcher's equipment, it is a dead ball, and all runners are awarded one base. Rule 5.09 g and 7.05 i.

The Right of Appeal

Billy Martin was a player who tried to turn negatives into positives. In a game in the mid-1950s, he checked his swing on an 0-2 pitch that bounced back to the screen.

Thinking that he might have broken the plane of the plate with his bat, he ran to first base, but was brought back to the batter's box by the home-plate umpire, who called the pitch a ball. Martin, not willing to give up a possible advantage too easily, appealed the call to the first-base umpire.

Does the first-base umpire rule or pass on the appeal?

Answer: He must pass. Only the defensive team may request an appeal. Rule 2.00: An appeal is the act of a fielder in claiming violation by the offensive team. The ball call stands.

Spectator Interference

The Oakland A's are losing by one run with two out and no one on base in the bottom of the ninth inning. Mark McGwire of the A's then hits a deep fly ball that clears the left fielder's reach and leaves the park for an apparent game-tying home run. But the left fielder claims that a spectator interfered with his making the catch.

What should the umpire do?

Answer: If the umpire saw the hindrance, he should rule the batter out for spectator interference and impose other suitable penalties. In this case, the A's couldn't win since there were no runners on base, McGwire would be declared out and the game would end with the A's losing by one run. Rule 3.16, APPROVED RULING.

In a real situation in the early 1960s, pinch-hitter Mickey Mantle of the Yankees was the batter, and Jackie Brandt of the Orioles was the left fielder. Mantle hit a dramatic home run that tied the game. Brandt argued that a fan had interfered with him. According to Brandt, he went back to the three-foot fence at Yankee Stadium and measured his leap to catch the ball. But the spectator, who was shielded from the umpires' view by the Orioles outfielder's body, slipped his hand around the back of Brandt's belt, and prevented his leap for the ball.

The umpires didn't see the spectator interference, however, and had to allow the game-tying blow to stand. The Yankees then won the game in extra innings.

Return to the Scene of the Crime

The Yankees have a runner on second base with two out and Don Mattingly at bat. Mattingly singles to left field. George Brett, the Kansas City Royal third baseman, senses that the Yankee runner at second base is going to score easily, so he cuts off the outfielder's throw to the plate and fires it to second baseman Frank White, who tags out Mattingly, who is attempting to pick up an extra base on the expected throw. Mattingly is the third out.

In the meantime, the runner who "scored" misses tagging the plate, but there is no appeal. Should the home-plate umpire draw attention to the runner's missing the plate? Suppose the runner who "scored" later returns to the "scene of the crime" and touches home plate?

Answer: The umpire should not draw attention to the runner's oversight. An appeal has to be requested by the defensive team. Rule 2.00 APPEAL.

In the late 1940s Joe DiMaggio once missed the plate on a play that was not followed by an out. But the Washington Senators, who were playing the Yankees that day, did not appeal the play, so the umpire said nothing and DiMaggio stealthily returned to the plate to touch it legally.

In the case cited here, the umpire's decision is based on whether the runner touched the plate before or after the third out. Rule 4.09a. Obviously he didn't touch at all, so if the defensive team appeals the play, the run doesn't count.

The Blacked-Out Game

Umpire Harry Wendelstedt was behind the plate in New York when the lights suddenly went out in the sixth inning during the notorious three-day blackout in the Northeast in 1977.

What is an umpire-in-chief's decision when he's standing in the dark?

Answer: The game is declared suspended with the action to be resumed from that point. Rule 4.12 [a-3]. The crew chief then documents the situation at the time of suspension.

When the lights went out at Shea Stadium in the above instance, there was a runner on first base. But when the game resumed at a later date, Wendelstedt noted that the runner had mysteriously advanced to third base.

"Oh no," Harry said, "we're not going to start that. You on third, first."

The players laughed. So did Wendelstedt. He didn't blame them for trying. Besides, he had the last laugh.

Foggy Play

Many remember the "Fog Bowl" between the Philadelphia Eagles and the Chicago Bears at Soldiers Field during the 1988-89 National Football League playoffs. League officials considered calling the game because of fog, but ultimately permitted it to continue. The Bears won.

A similar-type problem could—and has—occurred in baseball. Let us say that the Brewers and the Tigers are threatened with a fog-out at Milwaukee's County Stadium. What criteria for calling off the game might the umpires employ?

Answer: Visibility, of course, would be the key criterion. If the crew chief followed the precedent of umpire Frank Dascoli in a 1958 game, he would take his crew into the outfield and have a player hit a fungo fly ball. If neither the four umpires nor the three outfielders could see the ball, he would declare the game fogged out.

Gnatty Play

The Chicago Cubs have had games called under unusual circumstances. In a 1946 game against the host Dodgers at Ebbets Field, a swarm of gnats enveloped the field.

The day was sunny and the fans, who were annoyed with the gnats, tried to shoo them away with their white scorecards. The fluttering and flickering backdrop impaired the players' vision and endangered their safety, so the umpires called the game in the sixth inning.

Are games called under these or similar circumstances to be regarded as suspended, or are they handled like rainouts?

Answer: The fog-out and the bug-out were both treated like rain-outs. The Cubs-Braves fogged-out game was cancelled because the tied game had not gone five complete innings. Rule 4.10 e. The Chicago-Brooklyn game reverted back to the last complete inning, so the Dodgers won, 2-0.

Today when a game is called, the score at the moment of termination is the final score, except when the visiting team has scored one or more runs to tie the game, or has scored one or more runs to take the lead, and the home team has not scored to tie or take the lead. Rule 4.11 d: 1-2.

Out of Position?

The National League places its second-base umpire inside the bag, that is, on the edge of the infield grass, when there is a runner on first base, a runner on second base, or runners on all three bases. Otherwise, the Senior Circuit arbiter positions himself behind second base. The American League places its second-base umpire behind the bag on all plays, that is, on the edge of the outfield grass.

What are the respective merits of each placement?

Answer: National League umpires, most baseball people agree, are in the better position to call the steal and the force play. American League umpires, most baseball people concur, are in a better position to call the trapped ball in the outfield.

(Im)Perfect Play

When the field conditions are poor, the play is likely to be shoddy, too. Right?

Answer: Not necessarily.

Umpire Joe Paparella kept a September 20, 1958 game between the Yankees and the host Orioles going despite bad field conditions, because Baltimore had a good crowd, and he knew that the Birds could use the money. That was the day Hoyt Wilhelm pitched a 1-0 no-hitter against the Yankees. By the way, that's the last no-hitter that's been pitched against the Bombers. On the other hand, Don Larsen of the Yankees allowed just one hit in the six innings that he worked as a starting pitcher that day.

It was the best game that Paparella had ever worked, even though it probably shouldn't have been played.

The Left-Handed Apology

The Seattle pitcher who is working against Boston has a reputation of doctoring up the baseball. In the second inning of a contest between the two clubs, the home-plate umpire becomes convinced that the Mariner hurler has been throwing either a spitball or a greaseball.

Instead of searching the pitcher under suspicion, though, the umpire arbitrarily disallows a swinging third strike, claiming that the delivery was an illegal one, and gives the batter another chance to swing.

Can the umpire do that?

Answer: No, he can't, at least not according to Warren Giles, the former president of the National League. He took home-plate umpire Chris Pelekoudas to task for such a call. Pelekoudas made the call against Phil Regan, who was pitching for the Cubs at the time. Pete Rose of the Reds became the recipient of the extra swing.

Giles told Pelekoudas that the umpire was accusing Regan, of cheating without clear evidence. Pelekoudas ultimately apologized to Regan. Rule 8.02 [b-PENALTY -e].

Two Balls in Play

In a 1959 game between the Cardinals and the Cubs, Chicago pitcher Bob Anderson walked St. Louis batter Stan Musial. But the Bruin catcher argued with home-plate umpire Vic Delmore that Musial had fouled off the three-one pitch, which was then rolling to the backstop. When Musial noticed that the ball was not being retrieved by the catcher, he sprinted to second base.

In the meantime, third baseman Alvin Dark tracked down the loose ball and fired it to shortstop Ernie Banks, who was covering second base. During the preceding play umpire Delmore had unthinkingly given Anderson a new ball, and the pitcher, trying to throw out Musial at second base, sailed the throw into center field. Musial, who saw the ball rolling freely, decided to advance to third base, but Banks then tagged Musial out with the ball that Dark had thrown to him.

You've got two balls in play. What's the ruling?

Answer: Base umpire Bill Jackowski ruled Musial out because he was tagged with the original ball. The incensed Cardinals immediately protested, but they dropped their challenge after winning the game, 4-1.

Eyes in the Back of His Head

Let's zero in on a particular play in which a National League umpire, standing in front of second base, isn't in a position to make an informed call. Staring at the pitcher, who is standing off the area of the pitcher's mound, he doesn't see the Mets shortstop setting up the opposing runner at second base with the hidden-ball trick. The shortstop successfully pulls off the deception and makes a valid tag. Although the umpire has his back to the play, he wheels around after the fact and makes the right call.

The team that is at bat argues profusely, saying an umpire cannot call what he doesn't see.

Can he?

Answer: Yes, he can. A game between the Braves and the Giants at the Polo Grounds bears it out. Connie Ryan, second baseman for the Braves, pulled the play on Whitey Lockman of the Giants, who was called out. New York manager Leo Durocher argued vociferously. The umpire countered, "Didn't I get the call right?"

"Yes," Durocher said, "but you didn't see it, so you can't call it."

The umpire defended himself by saying, "I've got eyes in the back of my head."

But in reality what had happened was that he had looked at third-base umpire Al Barlick, who flashed him the out signal, and he in turn flashed the out signal to Lockman. The second-base umpire called the play through the eyes of the third-base arbiter.

Arm Signals

Why do umpires signal their calls with their arms?

Answer: William Ellsworth "Dummy" Hoy was a deaf, mute outfielder for seven teams around the turn of the Twentieth Century. He had a .288 lifetime batting average for 14 major-league seasons, and he stole 597 career bases. He was also responsible for the umpires raising their arms on ball-and-strike calls. Hoy couldn't hear the call, so he would turn around and look at the plate umpire. In time, the umpires started flashing him arm signals. It caught on.

What's the Score?

The Yankees are winning 1-0 in the top of the eighth inning when Don Mattingly hits a grand-slam home run. Then a huge downpour of rain causes the umpire to end the game. Is the final score 1-0 or 5-0?

Answer: It is 5-0. Mattingly gets to keep his four-run homer. The home run did not affect the outcome of the game. (The rule reverting back to the prior inning was changed in 1980.) If Mattingly's home run had modified the result and given the Yankees the lead, the game would have been suspended and replayed at a later date. And, if Mattingly's home run had been hit in the bottom half of the inning, the game would have been over, with the Yankees winning 5-0. Rule 4.11 d.

A Heady Play

In the bottom of the ninth inning, with the score tied, Tommy Herr of the Phillies is on first base with no out. On a hit-and-run play, Von Hayes smacks the ball behind Herr, and the spheroid caroms off the runner's helmet— which had fallen to the ground—and rolls down the right-field line. Herr rounds the bases and scores the apparent winning run.

Does it count?

Answer: Yes. A batted ball that accidentally strikes a helmet remains in play. The umpire views the play as if the ball had never hit the helmet. Rule 6.05. Paragraph beginning: "In cases where."

The Umpire's Mask

The Dodgers have the bases loaded with two out and a three-two count on the batter, Willie Randolph. Kit Gibson is on third base. Eddie Murray is on second, and Mike Scioscia is on first. On the pay-off pitch all three Dodger runners break with the delivery. Randolph swings at the pitch and misses, but the ball gets past the Phillies catcher and lodges in the umpire's mask. Before the catcher can extract the ball from the umpire's equipment, all three Dodger runners score, and Randolph gains third base.

Do the Dodgers really score three runs on this play? Suppose there had been less than two out at the time? Would that have affected the play?

Answer: First, only Gibson's run counts. The ball becomes dead as soon as it lodges in the umpire's mask. Randolph is awarded first base, and each runner advances one base. If the play had occurred with less than two out, Randolph would be automatically out, since first base was occupied at the time, but each runner would advance one base. Rule 5.09 g, 6.05 c, and 7.05 i.

Umpire's Error

Occasionally an umpire will make a mistake on the field that should not happen. For example, John McSherry, a very good arbiter, once called an infield fly with runners at second and third base and one out. Of course, for the umpire to rightfully make the call, runners have to be either on all three bases or on first and second base when a batter hits a catchable infield fly with less than two out.

What had happened in this instance was that there had been runners at first and second base and one out when a pitch evaded Mets catcher Jerry Grote. The runners each moved up one base, thus removing an infield fly situation. McSherry had somehow lost track of the runners' respective positions, though. So, lo and behold, he made a premature and illegal out call in front of 50,000 New York fans.

How did he get out of his predicament?

Answer: Well, he prayed. "Please, God, don't let Buddy Harleson drop this fly ball! C'mon, Buddy, atta-boy, Buddy!"

Fortunately, Harrelson caught the ball, so McSherry was left with a red face, but not a scarlet one.

Lightning Strikes Twice

The host California Angels are winning, 5-4, with the Seattle Mariners batting in the top of the ninth inning. Suddenly light failure halts the game. Then just before the lights are repaired, a lightning storm leaves the field in unplayable condition.

Is the game suspended. Or is it deemed a completed contest?

Answer: In this situation, weather takes precedence. It is a complete game. The Angels win, 5-4. Rule 4.11 d and 4.12 b-NOTE.

Shedding Some Light

Now that the Chicago Cubs have lights, baseball people at Wrigley Field have the opportunity to see both day and night baseball.

Let us say that the umpire-in-chief, during a rain-interrupted day game, orders the Cub technicians to turn on the lights in the bottom of the seventh inning. Mets manager Davey Johnson protests to the crew chief, citing discrimination. He says that if the lights are to be turned on, it should be done at the start of an inning, so that one team doesn't gain a distinct advantage over the other.

Is Johnson's protest a valid one?

Answer: No, it is not upheld. Of course, the umpire-in-chief should follow common courtesy in this regard, but he may legally turn the lights on at any time. Rule 4.14— The umpire-in-chief shall order the playing field lights turned on whenever, in his opinion, darkness makes further play in daylight hazardous.

Mental Mistake

The Blue Jays have Tony Fernandez on third base, George Bell on second base, one out, and a three-two count on Fred McGriff, who strikes out on the pay off pitch.

The Brewers catcher, thinking that there are three out, flips the ball to the umpire and walks toward the dugout. The umpire, momentarily confused, rolls the ball toward the mound while Fernandez and Bell both streak across the plate.

How does the home-plate umpire unravel this double mental mistake?

Answer: Very simple. He credits both runs. The umpire's handling of the ball doesn't affect Fernandez' and Bell's scoring on the play. Rule 5.08—It is the same as if the umpire had been hit accidentally by a thrown ball. The ball remains in play.

The Umpire's Offensive Assist

Kevin Bass of the Astros hits a hard ground ball that strikes an umpire who is standing behind the mound. The ball bounces off the umpire to Phillies second baseman Tommy Herr, who throws out Bass at first base.

Is Bass really out?

Answer: No. The ball becomes dead when it strikes the umpire under these circumstances. Bass receives credit for a single and is placed at first base. This is the ruling when a batted ball strikes an umpire in fair territory before touching a fielder. Rules 5.09 f and 6.08 d.

The Umpire's Defensive Assist

Suppose in the preceding scenario Bass's grounder got cleanly past the Phillie second baseman, hit the umpire behind the fielder, and then deflected to Herr, who threw out the runner at first base.

Would Bass be out then?

Answer: Yes. If a batted ball strikes an umpire after it passes a fielder other than the pitcher, it remains in play. Rule 6.08 d. Bass is out.

Quick Quiz

Here are umpiring situations that come up from time to time. See if you can make the right calls on these relatively simple situations.

• A ball is rolling in foul territory between home plate and first base. Before a fielder touches it, the ball hits a pebble and rolls back into fair ground where it comes to a stop. Fair or foul?

• Roberto Alomar hits a Baltimore chop; the ball hits home plate before it takes its first high hop. Alomar beats the play out at first. Is this a single, or should it be ruled a foul ball for hitting the plate?

• A grounder trickles through the right side of the infield, just inside the first base line. It barely eludes Will Clark of the Texas Rangers. In frustration Clark turns, takes off his mitt, and fires the glove at the ball. The mitt strikes the glove, causing it to roll foul near the right-field stands. Make your call.

Quotation

Marty Springfield had a rivalry with Earl Weaver. He once said, "That midget can barely see over the top of the dugout steps, and he claims he can see the pitches."

CHAPTER 9

Roadies and Rookies

Fun Facts

Life on the Trains

Players of the pre-airline era traveled long distances by train. Rookies were routinely assigned the worst sleeping quarters—upper berths on the last of the sleeper cars. Those were the cars that were the most unstable as they whipped around curves. After all, if anyone was going to get a bad case of mal de mer on land, it would be the lowly rooks.

Veterans would sometimes pull this one on rookies: The player chosen to be the "mark" would be told that there was a shoe thief on board the train. This opening gambit was credible back then, since players would leave their shoes on the floor outside their sleeping quarters when they went to bed. A porter would come along during the night and take the shoes away to have them polished. The rookie, though, didn't know about the shoeshine service, so he'd believe the tale of the mysterious thief.

The rookie was then told he'd have to stand guard and grab any suspicious characters lurking about. Sure enough, when the porter picked up a pair of shoes, the diligent rookie would grab the "culprit" while shouting excitedly about his great detective work. His reward was a chorus of laughter.

Boggs Speaks

Wade Boggs of Tampa Bay offered an explanation of the change in the treatment rookies receive today. Concerning their reaction to being treated like peons, Boggs said, "It's probably less tolerated by rookies now. They get a little bit more offensive more often [nowadays]. I don't know when the transition period [to that attitude] happened, probably in 1991 and 1992.

"Rookies get to the big leagues and sort of have an attitude that they've been here ten years. When I came up [in 1982 at the age of 24] with [Carl] Yastrzemski, [Mike] Torrez, [Dennis] Eckersley, [Jerry] Remy, and that type of individual [established veterans], it was a lot different.

"Rookies are to been seen and not heard," the six-time batting champ continued. "You keep your mouth shut. You learn your business, go about it, and put your time in. I think that's a lost art of paying your dues and keeping your mouth shut.

"I'm sure their money [big contracts now] has changed their attitude," he stated. He suggested that because Tampa Bay was an expansion club, things were a bit different. With so many young players, it's almost as if the whole team is made of rookies. In fact, 16 of the 40 players on their start-of-the-season roster were listed as first-year players. Boggs could report, then, that "The kids around here are very hard workers, willing to learn and have respect for the veterans."

Long Ago

From Boggs and his overview of the way things were and how they are now, let's flash back to long ago. In the old days, a rookie would not only get hazed, become the target of pranks and be tormented by teammates, he might even encounter treasonous behavior.

There's a story of a veteran catcher from the early days of baseball who had little regard for upstart, rookie hurlers. They say that the catcher, in situations which weren't crucial (such as two outs and nobody aboard), would actually tip off opposing batters as to what pitch was coming. He'd call for, say, a fastball, and then he'd whisper to the batter that a juicy fastball was coming down the pipe. It would have been tough enough for a hurler to face a veteran batter without the batter knowing what's coming, but prankish "treason" was the plight of some rookies way back when.

More on the Good Ol' Days

Long ago, veterans would nail a rookie's spikes to the club-house floor. This trick not only wouldn't be played today, it couldn't be done because of the plush carpeting in most clubhouses. Giving a rookie (or any teammate, for that matter) a hot foot was popular back in the days of the dead ball.

Ray Miller recalled how veterans would "nail their shoes to their locker, juvenile stuff." It may be puerile, but that's the nature of such ribbing.

Even Pittsburgh Hall of Fame shortstop Honus Wagner was chased out of the batting cage by veterans. Other greats such as Babe Ruth and Lou Gehrig got similar treatment. Ruth would go to the bat rack for a favorite bat only to discover the handle had been sawed off. Gehrig's bats were once sawed into four parts. On one occasion, Joe Bush, a teammate, called Gehrig "a stupid college punk," and there was no teasing in that voice. Carl Mays was also particularly cruel to Gehrig.

One reason veterans in baseball's early days were so abusive was that they were afraid youngsters would take their jobs or the jobs of their friends.

Phenom Number One

David Clyde broke into the majors in 1973 with the Texas Rangers, accompanied by Texas-sized hype. The ink was still wet on this 18-year-old's high school diploma when he made his big league debut. The fans' initial reaction to Clyde was not unlike what would happen three years later in Detroit with Mark "The Bird" Fidrych. Attendance boomed for the last-place Rangers, and the front office was understandably happy. (At least for the time being—Clyde went 4-8 and never really panned out.)

Despite all this, Clyde was treated with contempt by veterans. One teammate said, "Don't think I'm going to be your friend, because you're out after my job." And those were the first words immediately after the two players met!

Phenom Number Two

Wilson Alvarez also had an interesting start to his career. He threw a no-hitter in his first start with the White Sox. Despite such glory, he was treated like a typical rookie. "I always was the last guy to get to do things [such as hit in the batting cage]," Alvarez said. "It was, 'Get out of the way. Let me do my job first, and you do it after.' But I understood that. The guys who had been in the league for a long time need to work, and we'd respect that."

More Train (and Boat) Tales

Rookies weren't experienced in the ways of the world in the early days. One player, traveling by boat from New York to Boston, was conned into wearing a life preserver when he went to bed. He slept very fitfully.

Then there's the famous story of Babe Ruth's first train ride. He was on a train headed from Baltimore to Fayetteville as a member of the Orioles. The veterans looked upon him as a naive and overgrown child, so they gave him the then-common nick name "Babe." (Other "naming" stories exist, including one connected with Ed Barrow.) They made sure that Ruth spent his first night in an embarrassing posture.

Next to each Pullman upper berth was a sort of small hammock for players to place their clothes in. However, veteran Ben Egan told Ruth that its real purpose was for pitchers to rest their throwing arms. Ruth said the hammock held his arm in an uncomfortable position all night and that he went sleepless as a result. But, he figured, if that's what a big leaguer does, then so be it.

The result was humiliation and a very stiff arm the next day. Ruth called it "the first Oriole injury of 1914." He later said he had fallen for the oldest gag in baseball.

Dick Williams, the only manager to guide three different teams to the World Series, summed it up, "If you go way back, it was very tough on a first-year man. Now it's more business-like. The money is better, but they have less fun now."

Practical Jokes

Williams recalled another practical joke: "Someone would leave a message in the player's box telling him to report early for extra hitting the next day." Of course, the duped youngster would show up, but he'd be all alone.

Jay Johnstone, a legendary prankster who roamed the outfields from 1966 to 1985, used a similar joke. He'd send an official-looking letter to a raw rookie instructing him to appear at, say, a local television station for an interview. The rookie would beam with self-satisfaction until later, when he realized he'd been had.

The Red Baron Strikes Again

Rick "The Red Baron" Sutcliffe not only won a Cy Young trophy, he deserved the title "Prince of Pranks" as well. As a member of the Cubs in 1991, Sutcliffe was in the dugout when catcher Erik Pappas gathered his first big league hit. Sutcliffe retrieved the ball that had been underhanded into the dugout for safekeeping.

Realizing Pappas would want to preserve the souvenir of this proud moment, Sutcliffe's devilish mind began to churn. He inscribed the date and Pappas's name on the ball. Then, when Pappas trotted into the dugout, the pitcher presented him with the prized trophy. However, according to Pappas, "He used an old ball instead of the real game ball from my first hit. He purposely spelled my name wrong." Pappas naturally thought Sutcliffe had defaced the ball for a gag. At least that was a mild trick and one that was easily rectified.

In 1998, the Indians played a similar joke on rookie Alex Ramirez. After banging out his first hit, the veterans gave him a fake souvenir ball that was muddy and grass-stained. Once they got the reaction they wanted, they told him the truth and gave him the bona fide ball.

Rookie Batboys

Even a rookie batboy won't escape tricks. Indians manager Mike Hargrove told the story of how Sutcliffe would send a batboy looking for the key to the batter's box. Everybody was in on the joke, and they'd send the kid on a sort of wild scavenger hunt from clubhouse to clubhouse. "Sometimes," said the manager, who won the A.L. pennant in 1995 and 1997, "we'd send a guy for a bag of knuckleballs or curveballs."

Did they truly fall for such stunts? "Sometimes," responded Hargrove with a smile. "It never hurt to try."

Lasorda/LaRussa Tag Team

In 1992, Oakland A's manager Tony LaRussa borrowed a favorite Tommy Lasorda gag. Kirk Dressen-dorfer's spring-training performance had earned him the fifth spot in the pitching rotation. Yet on April 1, the day of LaRussa's conniving, the rookie pitcher wasn't aware he had made the team. Not only that, he probably didn't have much confidence going into camp, because players who were assigned jersey numbers such as his '60' don't usually head up north with the big boys who comprise the 25-man roster.

Therefore, when LaRussa told Dressendorfer he had been cut from the team, the pitcher sadly jogged off the diamond. LaRussa later said, "It was an April Fools' joke. He went to clean out his locker. Dave Duncan [pitching coach] called him over to say good-bye." It was only then, after all the theatrics, that Dressendorfer heard some laughter and realized it was all a joke.

"It had me a little worried," he recalled. "Then I saw them laughing. I thought it was pretty cold." He's correct, of course. Humor at the expense of rookies has always been rather ruthless.

Poor House Humor

Back in 1975, pitcher Fritz Peterson kept things loose in the Indians' spring-training locker room. A teammate of his, Duane Kuiper, looked back on a favorite trick. "Cy Buynak [the clubhouse attendant] would leave the weekly bill for clubhouse dues, say for $30, on players' chairs," said Kuiper. "Fritz put a '1' in front of the '30' on the rookies' bills. They'd see it [as a bill for $130] and almost die! They didn't know anything, and they'd believe everything."

Physical Humor

Players today still execute the classic "three-man lift." Cleveland slugger Jim Thome explained how the Indians did it in 1994. "The older guys tricked [rookies] Manny Ramirez and Julian Tavares into lying down for the 'lift.' One of the guys said to Manny and Julian, 'I bet I can lift you two up,' " said Thome.

At that stage, the two players went along with it, getting down on the floor, one on either side of the veteran, who was bragging of his strongman prowess. Thome continued, "The three guys interlock hands, and usually the middle guy is the one who knows what's going on. So, when he's interlocked, the other two guys are trapped. That's when everybody comes up and lifts their shirts over their heads and puts baby powder and shaving cream on them. They even dumped trash on them. They can't go anywhere. That was the funniest thing I ever saw in baseball."

Variation on the Three-Man Theme

Fred Patek said players in his era, the 1960s and even earlier, loved the trick Jim Thome described. Patek remembered, "They [his Pirate teammates] almost got me twice." The first time, they got him using the conventional means. Then, the second time, "They said it had something to do with stretching. The equipment manager set it up. They told me Steve Blass was going to be the victim, but I saw him with some aftershave lotion, shaving cream, and Tuff Skin. That's when I caught on and took off."

Incidentally, some teams used worse torture ingredients than the Pirates did. Some spread nasty-smelling liniments or blistering-hot ointments all over first-year players.

Traditional Trick

In 1997, Pittsburgh rookies Jose Guillen and Jeff Granger were flabbergasted when two Chicago policemen entered the Pirates clubhouse at Wrigley Field. When the officers told the two players that they were under arrest, they became apoplectic. The policemen announced that Guillen and Granger were being charged with vandalism.

It seems they went along with a National League ritual requiring rookies to vandalize a famous Chicago statue of a general on horseback. The tradition involves painting the private parts of the horse using the rookies' team colors. Later Guillen would claim he knew it was all a gag. He also confessed he was guilty of going along with the ritual, saying "Every rookie has to do it."

As the prank continued, Granger actually asked if he could make his one phone call. Only then did the pranksters tell the partners-in-crime that it was all a joke.

From Vandalism
to Grand Theft Auto

Shane Monahan broke into the majors with the Seattle Mariners. During 1998, his rookie season, his veteran teammates played a unique prank on the outfielder. It seems the Mariners were staging a promotion called "Turn Ahead the Clock" as a variation on the nostalgic "Turn Back the Clock" day that many teams run.

Between innings, the Mariners gave prizes away to the fans. At one point, Seattle veterans arranged to have Monahan's 1996 Ford Explorer taken from the players' parking area and driven around the field. The public address announcer said they were giving the Explorer away and read the seat number of the winning fan.

The veterans went so far as to include the "winner" in on the trick. The "fan" began to leap up and down in excitement while Monahan began to panic. Finally, he spied a chuckling Ken Griffey, Jr., on the bench and the realization hit him—he had been had!

Orosco Speaks

Jesse Orosco broke into the majors in 1979, so he's seen it all. He commented, "Now when tricks happen, you would think the kids would've heard about them growing up, but they still get caught with them. Evidently, somebody's not really pass-ing history on. We're probably glad that they don't.

"I remember the mongoose trick they did in Cincinnati for a lot of years. You can do it tomorrow to somebody before batting practice, and I guarantee you you're gonna get somebody who hasn't heard about it growing up." The trick he alluded to starts by telling a rookie that there's a wild mongoose trapped inside a box in the clubhouse. Warily, the rube will approach the box and, as he gets close, a veteran releases the "mongoose" using a spring mechanism. A hairy-looking fake creature seems to bolt out of the box directly at the victim, who invariably recoils in fear.

Cross-Dressing

The treatment a rookie gets can depend upon his status. For example, Dwight Gooden was a big name by the time he made it to the majors with the New York Mets. He stated, "I was lucky, actually. They were pretty good with me." On the other hand, he related that when Ryan Thompson came over to the Mets in a trade for David Cone, "We made him wear a dress in Philadelphia because he's from that area. His family was there, and we hid his clothes so he had to wear a dress and high-heel shoes on the bus."

Wilson Alvarez had similar recollections. "The rookies were dressed in funny outfits, sometimes like a woman. They'd make them do that in New York and go out and sign autographs for the fans looking like that. Or they'd make them dress like that and have them walk through a mall," Alvarez remembered.

Pitcher Pete Harnisch went into more detail on the type of clothes rookies had to wear, citing, "wacky shoes, outdated, old-fashioned ones like platform shoes and bad suits—purple, whatever."

Pat Corrales said that things are similar in Atlanta, but he tacked on a few items to Harnisch's list: "Our rookies here have to wear an outfit, and they get some loud, ugly, late-'60s outfits—lime, purple, bell-bottoms, big lapel [shirts], ugly polyester stuff, and big thick platform shoes." The Braves, he said, make the rookies wear these outlandish clothes on their first road trip.

However, when Corrales broke in, there was no such levity. He echoed the words of Wade Boggs: "You kinda had to keep your mouth shut and do what you were told."

Meanwhile, Tampa Bay's Quinton McCracken tossed in a few more sartorial notes: "There's always the patented dressing them up in tutus and sitting in front of the plane [like that]. As a rookie, I took it in stride. It's a fun part of the game. It's part of the tradition of baseball."

Still More Sartorial Items

The 1995 Indians went a slightly different route when rookie Herbert Perry joined the team. Shortly after the last game of his first road trip to Toronto, he was about to get dressed when he noticed, "All of my clothes were missing from my locker. I had to wear these hobo clothes [thoughtfully provided by veterans] all the way back through the airport. I swear, I thought there was no way they [American customs officials] were going to let me back into the country."

During a 1998 interview, Rafael Palmeiro said, "Earlier this year, we played the Marlins, and they have a bunch of young guys, rookies. Their clubhouse was on the other side [of the field from their dugout], so they have to come through a tunnel, come through where we come out of our clubhouse doors. It was the funniest thing—there were 12 babies with nothing on but big diapers. It was half their team with these diapers." It was bad enough for them to have to parade around their own locker room dressed in that style, but to have to be on display for the opponents was unbelievable.

Of course, Chicago White Sox rookies probably think they have it even worse. The tradition there is to have Robin Ventura pick out superhero costumes for the first-year players to wear on chartered flights.

St. Louis Blues

Chris Chambliss also recalled typical tricks on rookies: "In St. Louis there was a tradition where they take the rookies and make them dress in different [wild and weird] clothes on road trips. One time, we did it after we lost a game, and that didn't go over too good, but not much of that happens anymore."

Wilson Alvarez agrees with Chambliss that the treatment of rookies has changed. "It's not like when I broke in," he said. "The last couple of years, it's changed a lot. Most of the guys are treated the same—like everybody else."

Yankee Point of View

Most of today's players and observers believe that not only are tricks on rookies milder than in the old days, but they also occur less frequently. Scott Brosius of the 1998 Yankees said, "Especially this team here, they don't do a lot of things like that. I've never seen anything out of the ordinary [here].

"I think the game's a little bit different now. The money that they make now is so much different, so some of those traditions have started to fade away," said Chris Chambliss.

He added that at times a rookie's ordeal was to serve the veterans when a group of players went out to eat. Now, he says, even eating out with a bunch of players is dying out. Players aren't together as much as they used to be, so "some of those pranks don't really exist anymore."

Chambliss also pointed out that in the old days, "the older guys got more swings [in the batting cage] than the rookies, but nowadays everybody gets the same amount of swings because batting practice is so structured."

As long ago as 1945, Ty Cobb said veterans gave him a hard time after newspapers gave him a lot of publicity in his rookie year. Veterans hazed him because they were jealous. Cobb stated that every time he'd leave his hat unguarded, someone would twist it into knots. Cobb added that it was just such maltreatment that turned him from being a mild-mannered player into a belligerent one.

However, Cobb believed that the way rookies were treated in the 1940s was "gentlemanly." It's interesting, though, that if you'd ask a player from any old era if they were treated well as a rookie, he'd emphatically say "No." So each generation thinks they had it the worst.

Bell Sounds Off

David Bell, a member of the 1998 Seattle Mariners, has baseball roots that go back to the 1950s. His grandfather, Gus, was a major leaguer, as was his father, Buddy. That makes the Bell family the second of just two three-generation baseball families (the other one is the Boone family, which featured Ray, his son Bob, and grandchildren Aaron and Bret).

At any rate, Bell has a theory about why rookies were treated a lot rougher in the old days. "Maybe guys stayed with a team longer, and they developed more of a close-knit thing where you had to break into their circle." Bell, who once wore a skirt, much to the delight of Cardinal veterans, agrees with today's consensus, saying, "Guys are easier on rookies now."

Umpires Also Guilty

Maybe David Bell is correct, but Kevin Stocker feels umpires aren't as tolerant of rookies as they are of veterans. He feels that umps don't seem to give first-year players a fair shake. The Devil Rays played Atlanta in a 1998 contest featuring a marquee pitchers' duel. The Braves sent perennial Cy Young winner Greg Maddux to the mound to face rookie sensation Rolando Arrojo, who would shortly be named to the All-Star team.

Said Stocker of the duel, "It's not that simple. It's Maddux and the umpire against Arrojo and the umpire." Translation: The home plate umpire was a different man, or at least he called the game as if he were two different men, depending upon which pitcher was throwing. "Maddux gets another four inches off the plate. It was tough to see Rolando not get calls. You have to realize, this is Maddux; Rolando is a rookie." So, while the double standard apparently does exist, it still seems unfair to poor rookies. But, after all, that is their destiny.

Joe Pepitone's Strange Experiences in the Japanese Leagues

Joe Pepitone, a native of Brooklyn, New York, who seemed to have Hall of Fame credentials from the get-go, spent 12 tumultuous seasons in the major leagues—the first eight with the New York Yankees (1962–1969) and the remaining with Houston, Chicago, and Atlanta of the National League. While with the Atlanta Braves early in the 1973 season, he became disenchanted with baseball and just plain quit.

Several Japanese teams courted Pepitone at this critical point, and, by mid-June, Pepi had gotten the itch to play ball again. So he signed a lucrative two-year contract with Tokyo's Yakuruto Atoms, which belong to the well-regarded Japan Central League.

He made an auspicious debut on the night of June 23, when the Atoms faced the Tokyo Giants at Korakuen Stadium before a standing-room-only crowd of more than 45,000 superenthusiastic baseball fans. Pepitone's RBI single in the sixth inning proved to be the game's winning run as the Atoms edged out the powerful Giants 2-1. In the next several games, Pepitone played without distinction and reporters kept asking him when he was going to hit a home run. He finally did blast a long homer, a shot that proved to be another game winner. It was, unfortunately, Joe Pepitone's first and last homer in Japan.

Pepitone later recounted the dramatic events surrounding that game in Hiroshima: "I experienced the scariest moments of my life on the night I hit the homer. After that game, I got into a cab and I swear that more than 400 people surrounded the car. They started punching it and kicking it, and I thought I was finished. I had a bat with me. If I had used it, you would have seen another headline like 'Pepitone in Trouble Again.'"

The four-bagger even proved to be quite profitable. Pepitone said, "They do something in Japan I wish they'd do in the United States.... When you hit a homer in another park, the home team gives you presents—flowers, candy, clock radios, color TVs, and other good stuff. Your own team gives you a bonus of a couple of hundred bucks. Same thing if you drive in the winning run. The next day you get an envelope with money in it."

After the Hiroshima experience, Pepitone played in a few more games and then suddenly lost his desire to play anymore. He claimed that he'd injured his right ankle in a game and required both rest and medical attention. At this point, Pepitone had appeared in a total of 14 games, had gone to bat 43 times, had collected seven base hits (giving him a measly .163 batting average), scored only one run, and had batted in only the two game-winners described above. He never appeared in another game.

Management didn't believe Pepitone was hurt and ordered him to play. Through an interpreter, Atoms manager Hiroshi Arakawa told Pepitone, "You're a Japanese player now. You're not an American ballplayer. You play when we tell you to play."

Pepitone said of this incident, "That really got me teed. 'I'm not a Japanese ballplayer,' I told him. 'I'm a major leaguer.'"

The interpreter assigned to Pepitone by the Atoms, an Italian-Japanese named Luigi Ferdenza, stayed close to the recalcitrant first baseman just to make sure he didn't wander too far away. After all, the team had a great deal of money invested in him. "Everywhere I went, Luigi followed," Pepitone said.

About a week or so after he stopped playing, Pepitone sent his wife back home to Brooklyn and then moved in with Clete Boyer, his old New York Yankee teammate, who maintained a Tokyo apartment. Boyer, who adjusted well to Japan and Japanese baseball as the regular third baseman for Tokyo's Taiyo Whales, took Pepi under his wing, and agreed with the Atoms management that if the ankle was as seriously injured as Pepitone said it was, it should be placed in a cast.

Pepitone agreed and team doctors placed the ankle in a

cast, but then strange things began to happen. Within a short time the cast was removed, but not by the team doctors, and Pepi was allegedly seen dancing in several night-clubs near Tokyo's Ginza district. Just how serious the ankle "injury" was has never been clearly determined, but many felt there was reason to believe Joe Pepitone had been less than candid about the true nature of his physical condition.

The "disabled" first baseman spent his days in Boyer's apartment watching color television and calling his wife in Brooklyn. The overseas telephone charges for a month amounted to at least $3,000. Boyer has consistently maintained that Pepitone still owes him a very large chunk of it. Pepitone finally decided he could not "recover" from his "injury" in time to be of any use to the Atoms for the rest of 1973 and flew back home before the end of the season. "When the plane landed in the U.S.A., I kissed the ground," Pepitone declared.

The Atoms—or the Swallows, as the team is now called—were in a quandary over the whole affair, but they remained convinced that Pepitone could still be of value to them in 1974 and publicly announced early in the year that they fully expected him to report for spring training. The Japanese still had the elusive American signed to a two-year contract.

Spring training came and went, and nothing was heard from Pepitone. Marty Kuehnert, promotions director of the Taiheiyo Club Lions based in Fukuoka, and one of the balky Brooklynite's chief critics in Japan, commented in his monthly *Japanese Baseball Newsletter* for March 15, 1974: "The big question for 1974 is whether Pepitone will return to the Yakult Swallows .... It was really a shock to most fans when Yakult announced that they thought Pepitone was coming back this year. But Pepitone is up to his old tricks, and now it's a public joke as to whether he will or will not show. Apparently, Yakult's patience has grown thin. They are threatening to sever Joe's contract if he doesn't make it over soon."

In his newsletter for May 15, Kuehnert commented caustically, "Joe Pepitone has definitely been given up as a lost cause."

From his home in Brooklyn early in May, Pepitone began firing a volley of verbal salvos at Japanese baseball in general. His most scathing comments were contained in an article he wrote for the sports section of the Sunday *New York Times* for May 19, 1974. Pepitone opened his vitriolic essay by relating the unhappy thoughts he had when he was a discouraged $70,000 ballplayer (a lot of money in those days, incidentally) in the land of Nippon: "I'd wake up at three in the morning and kneel down next to the bed and pray, 'Please, God, don't let me die here.'"

Then Pepitone catalogued the misfortunes he endured in Japan during his brief tenure with the Atoms. "I just couldn't feel at home. No one spoke English, I tried to learn Japanese—right turn, left turn, straight ahead. I'd get into a cab and give directions, but if you didn't tell the driver in the exact accent, he didn't know what the hell you were talking about."

He went on to say, "But the playing part, it just wasn't major league. I had to carry my own bag. I never carried my own bag in the United States, and I wasn't going to start doing it in Japan."

Marty Kuehnert, in another of his newsletters, took Pepitone to task on the point. He wrote, "Pepitone complained that things in Japan just aren't 'Big League,' as he even had to carry his own bag. For the $70,000 Joe was paid, he should have carried the entire team's bags. It would have been more help than he gave the club on the field."

In his *New York Times* article, Pepitone complained about the high cost of living in Japan. He wrote, "If you wanted a McDonald's hamburger, it cost $5 . . . . When I moved in with Clete Boyer, we did some cooking. I stayed with Clete for a month. And you know what our grocery bill was for odds and ends like salt, pepper, and milk? It was $2,000. Those bonuses just weren't paying my way."

On the subject of the game itself, Pepitone remarked, "We had these team meetings before every game, and the manager gave these terrific pep talks in Japanese. I'd stand in the corner.... My heart just wasn't in this whole damn thing."

Pepitone's *Times* article caused a furor in Japan and was widely circulated throughout the country. It was reprinted in whole or in part in English-language dailies, including the *Asahi Evening News*, the *Daily Yomiuri*, and the *Mainichi Daily News*. The article was also translated into Japanese for many of the country's most important daily newspapers and sports weeklies.

Before and after his *Times* article appeared, Pepitone kept himself busily occupied with appearances on a wide number of New York radio and television shows—some of which were network broadcasts—and used these as a forum to repeat his criticisms of baseball in Japan and things Japanese.

The Japanese were deeply offended by the Pepitone diatribes, particularly those directly connected with pro baseball. Some Japanese, however, found elements of raw humor in the affair.

At a tea with Pacific League officials in the Asahi Building in the heart of Tokyo's Ginza district, when asked about the Brooklyn first baseman's contractual status with the Yakult Swallows, one of the executives exclaimed, "Joe Pepitone?" and then became semi-hysterical, laughing and crying at the same time.

Whenever we spoke with Japanese sportswriters or television and radio baseball announcers, they would almost inevitably ask, "What sort of fellow is this Joe Pepitone anyway?"

Pepitone, of course, wasn't at the ballpark long enough in Japan for anyone to really plumb the depths of his enigmatic personality.

Later on, Pepitone tried to get a major league team to sign him, but he failed in that quest because club owners doubted his reliability. After his experience in Japan, Pepi never played professionally again.

Over the years, Pepitone faced an array of personal problems, but in the late 1980s George Steinbrenner, owner of the New York Yankees, extended the hand of friendship to Pepi and gave him a part-time post in the team's promotions department. For over a decade now, Pepi has remained on the Yankees payroll.

In late spring 1998, we interviewed Clete Boyer at a Long Island card show and asked him if Pepitone had ever reimbursed him for the $3,000 worth of telephone charges made from his apartment in the summer of '73. Boyer rolled his eyes skyward and said, "I'm still waiting for my check."

Q&A

Resumed Games

Resumed games can be tricky. Take the following Reds-Expos game in 1986.

Going into the sixth inning, the two teams were tied in a 1-1 game. But in the top of the sixth inning, Kurt Stillwell of the Reds singled home a run off Montreal's Tim Burke to give Cincinnati a 2-1 lead. Then rain delayed the game and ultimately suspended it.

Why didn't the Reds get a 2-1 win?

Answer: In such a situation, when the visiting team goes ahead in the top half of the inning, the home team has to get its chance at bat, or the game has to be suspended and completed at a later date. Rule 4.11 [d-2]. Since the Reds didn't have another scheduled game in Montreal, the game had to be finished in Cincinnati. On the surface that seems unfair to the Expos, but the Reds, playing in their own park, continued to be the visiting team. As the game turned out, Dave Parker of the Reds hit a grand-slam home run, and Cincinnati won 10-2.

Index